To Paul;

In Hö

From
Glory to Glory

From Glory to Glory

WATCHMAN NEE
Translated from the Chinese

Christian Fellowship Publishers, Inc.
New York

Available from the Publishers at:

11515 Allecingie Parkway
Richmond, Virginia 23235

PRINTED IN U.S.A.

TRANSLATOR'S PREFACE

The glory of the Lord is not only in His person, but also in His work. Though glory is His dwelling, He divests himself of glory and takes up a humble fashion as a man. He endures the shame of the cross for fallen mankind, and nowhere does His moral glory shine brighter than on the cross. By means of His finished work at Calvary, the Lord Jesus is able to bring many sons to glory (Heb. 2.10). It is His prayerful desire that we may behold His glory (see John 17.24). And "we all, with unveiled face beholding as in a mirror the glory of the Lord, are transformed into the same image from glory to glory, even as from the Lord the Spirit" (2 Cor. 3.18).

In this present volume Watchman Nee interprets for us what is meant by the phrase, "from glory to glory." He begins with the name of Jehovah—the glorious name of God—and shows that man's only sin is falling short of God's glory. Yet God is so ready to forgive, although His forgiveness must be received by faith. He then cites the case of David and Mephibosheth to illustrate the mercy of God. The author further demonstrates the riches of God's grace by reviewing with us the salvation which comes through baptism, the food with which God provides His own, and a believer's value before God. By way of conclusion, He assures us of the love of Christ which is ever available to us and exhorts us to have the mind of Christ—which is indeed from glory to glory.

CONTENTS

1 | Jehovah

Moses said unto God, Behold, when I come unto the
children of Israel, and shall say unto them, The God of
your fathers hath sent me unto you; and they shall say
to me, What is his name? what shall I say unto them?
And God said unto Moses, I AM THAT I AM: and he said,
Thus shalt thou say unto the children of Israel, I AM hath
sent me unto you. And God said moreover unto Moses,
Thus shalt thou say unto the children of Israel, Jehovah,
the God of your fathers, the God of Abraham, the God
of Isaac, and the God of Jacob, hath sent me unto you:
this is my name for ever, and this is my memorial unto
all generations. Go, and gather the elders of Israel
together, and say unto them, Jehovah, the God of your
fathers, the God of Abraham, of Isaac, and of Jacob, hath
appeared unto me, saying, I have surely visited you, and
seen that which is done to you in Egypt: and I have said,
I will bring you up out of the affliction of Egypt unto
the land of the Canaanite, and the Hittite, and the
Amorite, and the Perizzite, and the Hivite, and the

Jebusite, unto a land flowing with milk and honey. And they shall hearken to thy voice: and thou shalt come, thou and the elders of Israel, unto the king of Egypt, and ye shall say unto him, Jehovah, the God of the Hebrews, hath met with us: and now let us go, we pray thee, three days' journey into the wilderness, that we may sacrifice to Jehovah our God. (Ex. 3.13–18)

God and Jehovah

Let us note that the names of God in the Bible are never used casually. Each time a certain name is employed, it has its special meaning. So are the names of the Lord Jesus in the New Testament; for example, none of the names such as Jesus Christ, Christ Jesus, the Lord Jesus Christ, and so forth can be changed within the context in which it appears. If we were to change Jesus Christ to Christ Jesus, we might commit a doctrinal error. And such is the nature of the revealed names of God that besides that of "God" itself He employs the name of "Jehovah" to express His relationship with the children of Israel. What is the distinction between God and Jehovah? By looking at the way in which God uses His name to reveal His own self, we may come to an understanding of these names.

From Genesis to the third chapter of Exodus, God employs various names by which to disclose himself. He uses at least three different names. In Genesis 1, we have the name "God." In Genesis 2, we have the name "Jehovah God." Why in the first instance is God used and in the latter instance Jehovah God is used? Is it not strange that God had not explained to anyone the meaning of this name? Abraham knew it because God had told him that His name was Jehovah, but Abraham did not know what it meant. Not until the time of Exodus 3.14,15 does God explain the meaning of "Jehovah" to men.

Why is it that Genesis 1 only uses God, and not Jehovah God? According to the original, the word "God" — "Elohim" in the Hebrew — means primarily "the Strong One." This name of God is employed in respect of the creation, for it speaks of God's relationship to creation. Jehovah, on the other hand, is God's name in relation to man. So that in Genesis 2 God's relationship to man is spoken of, and hence immediately the name Jehovah is introduced. The emphasis in Genesis 1 is creation (for man is not created until the sixth day); therefore the name "God" is used. Genesis 2, however, centers on man, and hence the name "Jehovah God" appears. Each time the term Jehovah God is used, it shows God's relationship with man. But each time the term God appears, it is to express His power as well as His relationship towards creation. Let us look at a few passages to show this distinction.

"They that went in, went in male and female of all flesh, as *God* commanded him: and *Jehovah* shut him in" (Gen. 7.16). Do you notice the distinction here? All that went into the ark went in male and female according to what *God* had commanded, but it was *Jehovah* who shut Noah into the ark. Can these names be reversed? No. He who commands is God, for command is related to the power of Deity. Therefore the word "God" is used. But now man came into the ark, and so the record tells us that it was "Jehovah" who shut him inside because the act of being shut in is expressive of the care of Deity.

"This day will *Jehovah* deliver thee into my hand; and I will smite thee, and take thy head from off thee; and I will give the dead bodies of the host of the Philistines this day unto the birds of the heavens, and to the wild beasts of the earth; that all the earth may know that there is a *God* in Israel" (1 Sam. 17.46). It says here that "Jehovah" will deliver the enemy into my hand that all the earth may know that there is a "God" in Israel. It does not say God will deliver an enemy into my hand that all the earth may know "Jehovah." Why? Because Jehovah is related to me. He looks after me and delivers the enemy into my hand. But with respect to all the earth—that is to say, to all the peoples outside the commonwealth of Israel—God does not reveal himself to them as Jehovah, but only as God. "Jehovah" is associated with those who are near to Him, whereas "God" is connected with the rest of the people in causing them to know His power.

"It came to pass, when the captains of the chariots saw Jehoshaphat, that they said, It is the king of Israel. Therefore they turned about to fight against him: but Jehoshaphat cried out, and *Jehovah* helped him; and *God* moved them to depart from him" (2 Chron. 18.31). He who helped Jehoshaphat was Jehovah, but He who moved his enemies to depart the scene was God. "Jehovah" helped Jehoshaphat because the latter was close to God, but in relation to the enemies the name of "God" was used since they had no communication with the Creator.

"God" is the common name of Deity, whereas

"Jehovah" is His intimate name. The term God speaks of Deity's power, while the term Jehovah speaks of Deity's love. The word God points to His creation, but the word Jehovah points to His nearness. In Genesis 1 the name Jehovah is not used because this passage relates the story of creation. Though it also mentions man, it nevertheless pertains primarily to God's creative power. In Genesis 2, though, it is recorded how God and man have intimate relationship; therefore, the name Jehovah God is employed. Why were not simply Jehovah and Jehovah God used instead? Let me say that this proves that the Jehovah in chapter 2 is the same One as the God mentioned in chapter 1. For Jehovah God is not only powerful but also approachable. In spite of the fact that the name Jehovah is employed thereafter, it is still not explained until the time of Exodus 3.14.

"I am Jehovah"

"God said unto Moses, I AM THAT I AM: and he said, Thus shalt thou say unto the children of Israel, I AM hath sent me unto you. And God said moreover unto Moses, Thus shalt thou say unto the children of Israel, Jehovah, the God of your fathers, the God of Abraham, the God of Isaac, and the God of Jacob, hath sent me unto you: this is my name for ever, and this is my memorial unto all generations" (Ex. 3.14,15). Moses had asked God: "Behold, when I come unto the children of Israel, and shall say unto them, The God of your fathers hath sent me unto you; and they shall say to me, What is his name? what shall I say unto them?"

And God had answered with this: "I AM THAT I AM [that is to say, Jehovah] . . . hath sent me unto you"! The primary meaning of the name Jehovah is "the self-existent One"—"He that is who He is, therefore the eternal I AM."

"I AM"—"I AM THAT I AM!" Oh! Do we realize the preciousness of that name? Do we truly know that "God is?" What He utters is great, what He leaves unuttered is equally great. When He speaks fully it is wonderful; when He speaks partially it is also wonderful. When He declares plainly it is marvelous, but when He discloses hesitantly it is just as marvelous. Here He does not fully reveal what He is; He merely says "I AM . . ." Hence the meaning is not complete. The "I AM" sent me. This is the revelation of God which Moses received that day.

If God were to add "power" onto the name "I AM," then His revealed name could not bespeak "love." If He were to add "love" onto "I AM," then His name could also not bespeak of himself as "power" or "wisdom" or "righteousness" or "sanctification" or "redemption" or "comfort" or "fortress" or "high tower" or "refuge" or whatever. And so He simply said to Moses, "I AM . . . ," without it stating what He is. God thus leaves this to the believers to add to it (and let me say that this is not mere letter, this is spiritual reality). We may fill in what God left unsaid according to faith. If we have faith as well as need, we may complete the "sentence-name" of "I AM" with whatever our need is, and we shall be supplied by God. If, for example, we are in need of comfort, then God can be to us as our comfort. If we are in need of refuge, He by faith can become our refuge. If in need of a high tower, then by faith He is our high tower. If in need of victory, He is our victory. If we are in need of holiness, then He can be our holiness. If we need light, then by faith He is to us our light. And if we need the bread of life, He is that to us too. Whatever be the need, we may fill that in by adding that to His name. We have no doubt that we may fill in whatever we need. It is not unlike a checkbook with an authorized signature already signed on every check and given to us. We may fill in whatever amount we need, whether it is a thousand or ten thousands of dollars. We simply fill in the amount of our need, because the signature is already there. How unfortunate that there are so many who do not really know who God is—so many who do not realize what Jehovah can be to them! Yet I see the breadth and length and height and depth of that name Jehovah! It truly includes *everything*.

No wonder those who know God take His name as a strong tower into which the righteous can run and are safe. Once we too have recognized this name, will we not also say with David, "They that know thy name will put their trust in thee" (Ps. 9.10)? The Old Testament saints knew God as Jehovah, and therefore they prayed: "For thy name's sake, O Jehovah, pardon mine iniquity, for it is great" (Ps. 25.11); "Save me, O God, by thy name" (Ps. 54.1); and, "Deal thou with me, O Jehovah the Lord, for thy name's sake" (Ps. 109.21). Therefore they could declare: "Through thy name will we tread them under that rise up against us" (Ps. 44.5); "He guideth me in the paths of righteousness for his name's sake" (Ps. 23.3); and, "I will lift up my hands in thy name" (Ps. 63.4). Therefore they could praise: "As is thy name, O God, so is thy praise unto the ends of the earth" (Ps. 48.10); and, "Sing unto God, sing praises to his name . . . his name is Jehovah" (Ps. 68.4). God himself has declared: "I will set him on high, because he hath known my name" (Ps. 91.14).

God's name reveals himself. His very name is the foundation of our faith. We will be able to do valiantly in God's name if we can enter into the reality of His name in the power of the Holy Spirit.

The Lord Jesus Is Jehovah

Some may consider Jehovah to be God's revelation in the Old Testament and therefore wonder if the New Testament people can enjoy the same benefits of that name. We thank and praise God because the Old Testament Jehovah is also the New Testament Jesus. The meaning of Jesus, in fact, is "Jehovah the Savior."

While on earth the Lord Jesus acknowledged himself to be the Jehovah of the Old Testament: "Except ye believe that I AM, ye shall die in your sins" (John 8.24). He told us here that He is the "I AM." Further on He also said this: "When ye have lifted up the Son of man, then shall ye know that I AM" (v.28); and again: "Verily, verily, I say unto you, Before Abraham was born, I AM" (v.58). He clearly declared that He is Jehovah, and the Jews themselves understood it, for it was because of this statement that "they took up stones . . . to cast at him" (v.59). Let us rejoice, for our Lord Jesus is the great I AM. HE IS! For our sakes, He is! He himself announces: I am the life, I am the resurrection, I am the light of the world, I am the bread of life, I am the good shepherd. We may receive all our supplies in the name of our Lord Jesus — Jehovah the Savior! When we have His name, we have everything. How we thank Him for giving His name to us.

Jehovah

"Go, and gather the elders of Israel together, and say unto them, Jehovah, the God of your fathers, the God of Abraham, of Isaac, and of Jacob, hath appeared unto me, saying, I have surely visited you, and seen that which is done to you in Egypt: and I have said, I will bring you up out of the affliction of Egypt unto the land of the Canaanite, . . . unto a land flowing with milk and honey" (Ex. 3.16,17). This name Jehovah was used especially during the period from the Exodus to the entering in of Canaan. Throughout this time, this name was frequently employed. Hence, from the day in which we are saved to the time in which we inherit the kingdom — and however difficult our paths may be — Jehovah is our great I AM. His name shall lead us to the end. The name Jehovah is not God's name relative to creation, but is His intimate name for the believers in the wilderness. It enables us to pass through the wilderness and enter the Promised Land.

Believers' Responsibility

What is the effect of this name of Jehovah in relation to the children of Israel? That they might take up their responsibility before God.

God will not argue, for if He does, who can answer Him? His reason is often beyond our understanding, since He himself is the reason. Let us illustrate from Scripture this that we have just said (all from Leviticus, except where noted):

> Mine ordinances shall ye do, and my statutes shall ye keep, to walk therein: I am Jehovah your God. (18.4)
>
> Ye shall therefore keep my statutes, and mine ordinances; which if a man do, he shall live in them: I am Jehovah. (18.5)
>
> I am Jehovah. (18.6b)
>
> I am Jehovah. (18.30b)
>
> Speak unto all the congregation of the children of Israel, and say unto them, Ye shall be holy; for I Jehovah your God am holy. (19.2)
>
> Turn ye not unto idols, nor make to yourselves molten gods: I am Jehovah your God. (19.4)
>
> Thou shalt not glean thy vineyard, neither shalt thou gather the fallen fruit of thy vineyard; thou shalt leave them for the poor and for the sojourner: I am Jehovah your God. (19.10)
>
> Ye shall not swear by my name falsely, and profane the name of thy God: I am Jehovah. (19.12)
>
> Thou shalt not curse the deaf, nor put a stumbling block before the blind; but thou shalt fear thy God: I am Jehovah. (19.14)
>
> Thou shalt not go up and down as a talebearer among thy people: neither shalt thou stand against the blood of thy neighbor: I am Jehovah. (19.16)
>
> Thou shalt not take vengeance, nor bear any grudge against the children of thy people; but thou shalt love thy neighbor as thyself: I am Jehovah. (19.18)
>
> I am Jehovah thy God. (19.25b)

Ye shall not make any cuttings in your flesh for the dead, nor print any marks upon you: I am Jehovah. (19.28)

Ye shall keep my sabbaths, and reverence my sanctuary: I am Jehovah. (19.30)

Turn ye not unto them that have familiar spirits, nor unto the wizards; seek them not out, to be defiled by them: I am Jehovah your God. (19.31)

Thou shalt rise up before the hoary head, and honor the face of the old man, and thou shalt fear thy God: I am Jehovah. (19.32)

The stranger that sojourneth with you shall be unto you as the home-born among you, and thou shalt love him as thyself; for ye were sojourners in the land of Egypt: I am Jehovah your God. (19.34)

Ye shall observe all my statutes, and all mine ordinances, and do them: I am Jehovah. (19.37)

Thou shalt take the Levites for me (I am Jehovah) instead of all the first-born among the children of Israel; and the cattle of the Levites instead of all the firstlings among the cattle of the children of Israel. (Num. 3.41)

Take the Levites instead of all the first-born among the children of Israel, and the cattle of the Levites instead of their cattle; and the Levites shall be mine: I am Jehovah. (Num. 3.45)

Do God's commands have a reason behind them? Only that it is because "I am Jehovah." No other reason than this is given to explain God's various commands here. I will chastise you because I am Jehovah. I will take the Levites for myself. Is this because the children of Israel defraud Me? No, but because I am Jehovah. You must not curse the deaf, because I am Jehovah. You cannot do this or that, because I am Jehovah. Continually, there is no other reason put forward. How blessed a person is if he will obey simply because God says "I am Jehovah." There are plenty of reasons in the world to induce a person to sin, but blessed is he who will not sin simply because God is the I AM.

To put it more clearly, however, the name of God as the "I AM THAT I AM" shows us at least two reasons for His commands: (1) "I AM" —that is to say, I am powerful, therefore you should not do anything. I am your power, protection, holiness, righteousness and supply. Hence you have no need to sin. You say you have passions and lusts in you, but Jehovah declares: "I am righteousness and holiness." So why must you sin? You say you have no money, so you ask for a loan; but Jehovah says to you: "I am your supply. Hence why should you borrow? Therefore, if you sin, it is not because I cannot help you or keep you from sinning. I am indeed able to keep you. But you sin because you want to sin."

(2) "I AM"—that is to say, I am not only your power and wisdom who loves you dearly and has chosen you, I am also Jehovah your God who will chasten you if you do evilly. So that, yes, the I AM is first of all powerful; but second of all, He will judge. First, He is most powerful in being our righteousness and holiness; but next, He will judge us according to His righteousness and holiness. When He uses this name of Jehovah— the I AM THAT I AM—He does not bother to explain the reason for His commandments. He simply tells His people, "I am Jehovah." I am Jehovah who brought you into Canaan. I am Jehovah, therefore you must do or not do these various things.

"I am the God of Abraham, the God of Isaac, and the God of Jacob"

"God said moreover unto Moses, Thus shalt thou say unto the children of Israel, Jehovah, the God of your fathers, the God of Abraham, the God of Isaac, and the God of Jacob, hath sent me unto you: this is my name for ever, and this is my memorial unto all generations" (Ex. 3.15).

Here an additional explanation is being given. Who is this Jehovah your God? He is the God of Abraham, of Isaac, and of Jacob. So far as *God himself* is concerned, He is Jehovah, the I AM. So far as *men* are concerned, though, Jehovah is the God of Abraham, of Isaac, and of Jacob. On Deity's side, He is God, He is Jehovah; this is what He has revealed to men. On men's side, God has revealed himself to Abraham, to Isaac, and to Jacob; and this is to cause us to see what power He will manifest in *our* lives just as He has manifested His power in those men.

Why does God not declare himself as the God of Adam? For we know that Abraham sinned even as Adam did. Why then did He not call himself the God of Adam? Why did He not say the God of Abel, the seed of Adam? Why instead did He call himself the God of Abraham, of Isaac, and of Jacob? Why according to the flesh was our Lord Jesus presented in the New Testament as having been born of the seed of Abraham? Why from among all men should God have called himself the God of these three particular persons? Wherein lies the difference between these three and other people? Well, apart from the fact that God had covenanted with these three men, He takes them up as representative personages. He chooses them to represent three types of men in the world.

What type of man is Abraham? He is a giant of faith. He is rather uncommon; in fact, he is quite special. As the God of Abraham, God declares himself to be the God of excellent people. Yet, thanks be to God, He is not only the God of the excellent. Were He merely this kind of God, we would sink into despair because we are not persons of excellence. But God is also the God of Isaac. What type of person is Isaac? He is very ordinary. He eats whenever he can, and sleeps as he has opportunity. He is neither a wonder man nor a wicked person. How this fact has comforted many of us! Yet God is not only the God of the ordinary men, He is also the God of the bad men: He is the God of Jacob too, for in the Scriptures Jacob is pictured as one of the worst persons to be found in the Old Testament.

Hence through these three persons, God is telling us that He is the God of Abraham the best, the God of Isaac the ordinary, and the God of Jacob the worst. He is the God of those with great faith, He is the God of the common people, and He is also the God of the lowest of men such as thieves and prostitutes. Suppose I am special like Abraham; then He is my God. Suppose I am ordinary like Isaac, then He is also my God. And suppose from my mother's womb I have been bad like Jacob was in that I have striven with my brother; then He is still my God. He has a way with the excellent, with the common, and with the worst of humanity.

From that day in Exodus onward, God has always called himself by this wonderful name without any change. Even when the Lord Jesus was about to face death, He said this: "As touching the resurrection of the dead, have ye not read that which was spoken unto you by God, saying, I am the God of Abraham, and the God of Isaac, and the God of Jacob? God is not the God of the dead, but of the living" (Matt. 22.31,32). Here our Lord adds one more meaning to that name. When God calls himself by such a name, it reveals the fact that He is also the God of resurrection. However excellent Abraham may be, he is subject to death and decay; but God will cause him to be raised again from among the dead. As common as Isaac is, he too will die and decay; yet God will also raise him. And as bad as Jacob is, he also will die and decay; nonetheless, God will raise Him up too. In the realm of resurrection, all which belongs to the natural will pass away. God is the God of the living, not of the dead. So that in the resurrection realm, God is to be the God of these three men. This indicates to us Christians — and whether we are naturally talented, ordinary, or bad — that we will all decay; nevertheless, our God will re-create us and make us new in Him. Though we are so different in the natural, God will eliminate all the differences and be our God all the same. For what He looks at is not our natural endowment but the life He has given us. According to the natural, there exist vast differences among Abraham, Isaac, and Jacob; but in resurrection they all receive the same life. God overlooks the natural and looks only at His work of grace. He is able to dispense grace to totally different people and make them almost the same.

What is meant by resurrection? It means the natural

has passed away and the supernatural has come. Regardless the fact that some people are highly talented, that some are rather ordinary, and that some are tricky and bad, God in His Son can make all new. How useless is the natural, only the supernatural is profitable. For the eyes of God are focused on resurrection. And hence He can be the God of Abraham, of Isaac, and of Jacob.

Memorial Forever

"This is my name for ever, and this is my memorial unto all generations" (Ex. 3.15). This means "I eternally AM," that "in Me is the yea." Here the name Jehovah bespeaks two things of note: (1) I am forever Jehovah. As My name is, so shall I be for eternity. And (2) My memorial. Let Me be remembered as Jehovah to all generations. And I too will always remember I am Jehovah. Unless God forgets He is Jehovah and we forget He is Jehovah, God stands forever as is to us, and He will forever supply all our needs. Hallelujah!

2 | Man's Only Sin

Of the tree of the knowledge of good and evil, thou shalt not eat of it: for in the day that thou eatest thereof thou shalt surely die. (Gen. 2.17)

The man said, The woman whom thou gavest to be with me, she gave me of the tree, and I did eat. (Gen. 3.12)

Esau said unto Jacob, Feed me, I pray thee, with that same red pottage; for I am faint: therefore was his name called Edom. (Gen. 25.30)

I will arise and go to my father, and will say unto him, Father, I have sinned against heaven, and in thy sight. (Luke 15.18)

He that believeth on him is not judged: he that believeth not hath been judged already, because he hath not believed on the name of the only begotten Son of God. (John 3.18)

Of sin, because they believe not on me. (John 16.9)

Let all the house of Israel therefore know assuredly, that God hath made him both Lord and Christ, this Jesus whom ye crucified. Now when they heard this, they were

pricked in their heart, and said unto Peter and the rest
of the apostles, Brethren, what shall we do? And Peter
said unto them, Repent ye, and be baptized every one of
you in the name of Jesus Christ unto the remission of your
sins; and ye shall receive the gift of the Holy Spirit. (Acts
2.36-38)

Because that, knowing God, they glorified him not
as God, neither gave thanks; but became vain in their
reasonings, and their senseless heart was darkened. (Rom.
1.21)

Wherefore God gave them up in the lusts of their
hearts unto uncleanness, that their bodies should be
dishonored among themselves. (Rom. 1.24)

For this cause God gave them up unto vile passions:
for their women changed the natural use into that which
is against nature. (Rom. 1.26)

And even as they refused to have God in their
knowledge, God gave them up unto a reprobate mind, to
do those things which are not fitting. (Rom. 1.28)

As it is written, There is none righteous, no, not one.
(Rom. 3.10)

All have sinned, and fall short of the glory of God.
(Rom 3.23)

What I want to emphatically present is the only sin
in the Bible. It appears to be quite strange that the way
man looks at sin is totally different from the way God
looks at it. It is a pity today that in preaching the gospel,
people often incorrectly present the principle of sin.
Man is in need of a Savior because he has sinned. If
there were no sin, there would be no need for a Savior.
But *what* is the sin which man has committed? The

word sin is a generic term. You have your sin, and I have mine. If we therefore do not commit the same sin, then why do we all need the same Savior?

The Bible from the beginning to the end lays stress on but one sin. Whether a person receives eternal life or perishes depends on his attitude towards this one sin. His standing before God is determined by his treatment of this sin. The Bible does not stress tens of thousands of other sins. Even were all the tens of thousands of these other sins resolved, you would still be a sinner if this one particular sin were not solved in your life. What, then, is this sin? It is a controversy between man and God, that man *does not have a proper relationship with God.* Although lying, pride, and jealousy are all sins, these are merely bits and pieces of this one particular sin. What according to the Bible causes man to perish is but one particular sin. You may not commit many other sins, but if you commit this one, you are qualified indeed to descend to hell.

We may not commit adultery or gamble, but we doubtless have committed this one sin—which is the lack of a proper relationship with God. There may be a clean man or woman, but he or she has committed the sin of having a controversy with God. We have all committed this same sin of having broken the proper relationship with God. We are born sinners.

The inventory of sin is so massive that it is beyond counting. You may happen to have not committed any of the numberless sins in the world, yet there is one sin you cannot deny having committed—which is, that you have *broken off your relationship with God.* Without Christ today, you are indeed a sinner. What is sin? It is nothing less than man standing in a position of being unable to commune with God. To sin is basically to stand in a position opposed to God. Sin is more than murder or pride or jealousy: it is having a controversy with God.

Let me use an illustration to show how important such sin is. Suppose there is a man who is married and has children. He also has in his big family parents, brothers, and sisters. He is working, and naturally he has his colleagues where he works. He has in addition many relatives and friends. In his own home he may be a good husband and father. At his work he may be most diligent and faithful. He is loyal to his friends and does good towards his relatives. In fact, he is good in every respect. He does not smoke or drink; he tells no lie and is not jealous. He keeps all the commonly accepted moral codes. He is a real gentleman. Nonetheless, he has one peculiar aversion; he hates his parents. He is agreeable with everybody else except with them. He is courteous to all save his parents. He is easy on everyone but them. It can be said that he is moral and good to all, that he has not committed any of the gross sins which other people usually have done. Even so, he has committed a great sin — that of maintaining an improper relationship with his parents. He has not committed sins commonly perpetrated, yet he has committed this one grave sin of having a controversy with his parents.

Let me say that such is the position of the world of men today. When asked if they are sinners, many will answer back, How have I sinned? According to the human viewpoint, these who reply in such fashion are no doubt gentlemanly, moral, and polite. They seem also to follow their conscience well. Nevertheless, each of these people needs to be asked this question: Has anything bad happened between you and God? True, you have maintained a good relationship with friends and relatives, you are moral and courteous, but what about your relationship with the heavenly Father? Keep in mind that besides your wife, children, friends, and relatives, there is also God above towards whom you must relate.

Hence, we may accurately say that man is a sinner for no other reason than his having an improper relationship with God. It is not because he has killed people or his conscience is too black that he is constituted a sinner; he is such basically because he stands at enmity with God. He is a sinner because he has no spiritual intercourse with God. Man can make excuses by saying he has not committed this sin or that sin, but there is one particular sin which he *must* have committed. We each may put forth excuses to explain away a hundred and one other sins, but we cannot deny we have in fact committed this one sin. It is this sin that makes you and me sinners.

Today I would not ask concerning how you behave at home. Possibly you are a good member of your family. Neither would I ask if you are at peace with your brothers. Perhaps you have indeed not sued any of them because of some inheritance conflict. Nor would I ask you how you treat your colleagues at work. Your colleagues may well in fact respect and think highly of you. And I would not ask if you are a good citizen. Perhaps you are a very good one, for you are loyal, submissive to authority, and faithful in paying taxes. But I *would* ask you today if something is wrong in your relationship with God. What is your relationship with Him? God will not ask you how you behave towards your wife, brothers, and colleagues. He will not even ask you whether you have killed someone or committed arson. He will only ask you about your relationship with Him. You may not have created many other problems present in the world, but if this universally common problem of man's relationship with God is not resolved, you are nontheless a sinner.

The Bible teaches plainly concerning this sin. Let us be clear as to just exactly how sin first entered this world. It did not enter in the form of murder, nor a lie told by someone calling his wife his sister. It did not enter the world by a man having taken another's wife or having sent a rival to the battlefront to die. Nor did it enter through fornication or gambling or pride or jealousy. No, sin first entered the world quite simply by man having eaten a piece of fruit.

"Of the tree of the knowledge of good and evil," commanded God of Adam, "thou shalt not eat of it: for in the day that thou eatest thereof thou shalt surely die" (Gen. 2.17). We will not touch upon the reason that lay behind God's word here. We will merely observe that man overturned what God had commanded. If the Creator God orders me not to eat, then I shall not eat; otherwise I contradict and oppose God. Now as soon as Adam had eaten the forbidden fruit, he quickly hid himself among the trees of the garden since he had placed himself in a posture of fearing to see God. What, then, is sin? Sin is simply having a wrong relationship with God. Sin is standing in an improper position towards God.

It was doubtless sin for Cain to kill Abel; but before he had ever contemplated killing Abel, sin had already been present. God did not reject Cain *after* he murdered his brother; He had rejected him *beforehand*—when he had offered the produce of the field. Cain was rejected because his relationship with God was already wrong. Now he had actually thought of pleasing God when he decided to offer up the produce of his field. He could be termed what is today commonly known as being religious. Cain offered up the labor of his hands to God in order to please Him. But he had failed to see that sin was already present in the world, and that therefore the only position he could take would be to stand on the ground of the blood. He was thus rejected because he refused to stand on the ground of the blood. In other words, Cain's position was faulty.

We are all familiar with the story of the prodigal son in Luke 15. What was the sin he committed? Many would say, Look, the younger son took his share of his father's property and wasted it in riotous living, and thus he later became a prodigal. Let me say, however, that the day on which he received his inheritance into his hands was when he became a prodigal, even though he was a wealthy man at the moment. He became a prodigal not because he had failed, wasted all his inheritance, and fallen into feeding swine. The moment he left his father to go into a far country was the moment he became a prodigal. When he stepped out of his father's door, that was when he became a prodigal. His one fault that made him a prodigal was to leave his father. Yet suppose this younger son had become even more wealthy rather than poor abroad. Suppose that instead of having five thousand, he now had ten thousand dollars. His father could still not have said to him, Well done, good and faithful son. Even if he had become ten times richer, the younger son still remained a prodigal.

Hence the problem today is not whether one has spent all, or has resorted to feeding swine for a living, or has ended up hungry and in rags. The real problem is, where are you? Is there something wrong in your relationship with the heavenly Father? If you are in a far country, you must have become a prodigal son also. But when the prodigal in the Biblical account came to his senses, he did not plan to work hard and accumulate money so that he might turn from beggar to rich man. What did he say to himself when he was inwardly awakened? "I will arise and go to my father, and will say unto him, Father, I have sinned against heaven, and in thy sight" (Luke 15.18). He did not return just to satisfy his stomach with food and to have shoes and clothes to wear. He said, "I will arise and go back to my father."

What is meant by being saved? It means to have restored a proper relationship with God. What is eternal life? To have eternal life is to have a right relationship with God the Father: "this is life eternal, that they should know thee the only true God, and him whom thou didst send, even Jesus Christ" (John 17.3).

Had the younger son maintained a proper relationship with his father, he would not have left at all. Whoever leaves one's heavenly home is a prodigal son or daughter. Whoever leaves the Father in heaven is a prodigal. But when in the story the prodigal son returned home, he was to his father dead and now alive, lost and now found. So is it in the spiritual realm, too.

Hence, let us see that you and I became sinners not because we had committed so many different sins, but because we could not see God's face. I do not say these many sins are not sins with which we need to be concerned; I would only say that not to have a proper relationship with God is *the* sin.

In the first three chapters of Romans, Paul shows us most plainly the qualification of being a sinner. What makes one a sinner? How does he "earn his degree"? The sin of a sinner is none other than having a problem with God. Three times in the first chapter of Romans Paul mentions that "God gave them up." Let us look at each case.

"Because that, knowing God, they glorified him not as God, neither gave thanks; but became vain in their reasonings, and their senseless heart was darkened" (1.21). The "they" here points to men. Men know that God is God and yet they do not treat Him as God. They know He is God, but they do not glorify Him as God. All the many different sins which appear are not the root of sin; these come from the *one* sin, which is, that men do not respect God as God, and thus their reasoning becomes vain and their senseless heart is darkened to commit all kinds of sin.

"Wherefore God *gave* them *up* in the lusts of their hearts unto uncleanness, that their bodies should be dishonored among themselves" (1.24). "Wherefore" follows the preceding thought. Because men have turned the glory of God into creature likenesses, God therefore gives them up. Thus, they commit uncleannesses according to the lusts of their hearts. Let us recognize that men's first sin is not uncleanness according to the lusts of their hearts, neither is it a dishonoring of their bodies. The *first* sin which men commit is to be at odds with God. Allowing such a controversy to occur, men naturally will subsequently commit all the other sins. Today we consider lying, pride, jealousy, fornication, killing, and so forth to be heinous sins. Actually these are but symptoms, not the disease itself. Merely treating symptoms such as the treating of the head when there is a headache and the foot when there is foot pain is not reckoned as the mark of a good physician. A good physician will prescribe according to the cause of the disease. And in the spiritual realm, the one disease men have is that of having a problem with God himself.

"They exchanged the truth of God for a lie, and worshipped and served the creature rather than the Creator, who is blessed for ever. Amen" (1.25). This indicates that the farther away one is from God the worse the relationship with God becomes.

"For this cause God *gave* them *up* unto vile passions: for their women changed the natural use into that which is against nature" (1.26). "For this cause" again continues on with what precedes it. This is the second use of the phrase "gave up." The sins mankind commits have increased: "God gave them up unto vile passions." All this is because they do not honor the Creator. These sins are fruits, not the cause.

"And even as they refused to have God in their knowledge, God *gave* them *up* unto a reprobate mind, to do those things which are not fitting" (1.28). This is the third instance of the use of these two words "gave up." Even more sins are to be committed, as is evident in the verses that follow:

> Being filled with all unrighteousness, wickedness, covetousness, maliciousness; full of envy, murder, strife, deceit, malignity; whisperers, backbiters, hateful to God, insolent, haughty, boastful, inventors of evil things, disobedient to parents, without understanding, covenant-breakers, without natural affection, unmerciful: who, knowing the ordinance of God, that they that practice such things are worthy of death, not only do the same, but also consent with them that practice them. (1.29-32)

How do these numerous sins come about? All are due to the fact that men "refuse to have God in their knowledge." Men sin because they refuse to know God. Men sin because they have problems with Him. Once the relationship between man and God becomes improper, all kinds of sins quickly follow.

Once again we see that the one and only sin of man is his having a problem with God. The supreme question today is whether or not one's relationship with God is right. The first sin committed by the very first man was his eating fruit. There was no killing, no lying, no pride, fornication, or jealousy. None of these sins was present. Only one sin was committed—that of having an improper relationship with God. And as a consequence God was forced to ask man, "Where art thou?" (Gen. 3.9) So that today we do not stand on the original ground, but stand on an improper ground since our relationship with God is improper. And

because of this, numberless sins end up being committed. Let us never conclude that because we may have
dealt with some small sins, we are therefore somehow
all right. Not so.

Let me ask you who suppose you are not a sinner,
what is your relationship with God? I do not ask what
is your relationship with your brothers, wife, children,
friends, or colleagues. I merely ask what your relationship is with your Father. Cain at the very outset was
rejected by God because he stood on the wrong ground.
He was not rejected after he slew his brother; on the
contrary, Cain slew his brother because he had already
been rejected by God. On the other hand, because Abel
was accepted by God, he did not kill his brother Cain.
Only those who are accepted by God will not commit
sin.

There was once a man — told of in the Bible — who
fought with his brother even while in his mother's
womb. He later became most cunning. He cheated his
father and father-in-law. Whatever was advantageous
to him he did without hesitation. His morality was
tremendously low. Who was this man? Jacob, of course.
His brother Esau was rather candid. Though he had
vowed to kill his brother, nevertheless, when he saw his
brother's humility, he let him go. He was indeed the
better man of the two, yet God was not pleased with
him. Bad as Jacob was, he nonetheless had a proper
relationship with God. Though his means were deceitful, his aim was good. For he desired after the covenant which God had made with Abraham and Isaac.
He respected the birthright of the firstborn. Abraham
and Isaac had a right relationship with God because

God had made covenant with them. And Jacob sought for that too. Esau, on the other hand, appeared to be a gentleman who was willing to let go of everything, but he had lost contact with his God. He despised the relationship with God. He did not appreciate his position before Him, and thus he was unable to receive the inheritance (a type of the kingdom.) But Jacob, though deceitful, still had a proper relationship with God.

Let me openly acknowledge one thing here, which is, that among the believers there are many whose moral status falls behind that of worldly people. Yet I can testify for such believers that their relationship with God is proper. To you who are still unbelievers, let me say that you may be courteous and diligent, with everybody praising you; but I need to ask you one question: what is your relationship with God? Some believers may not morally be as high as you are, yet they exceed you in one very important respect, which is, that their relationship with God is right whereas yours is not. We believers can approach God with boldness and without fear in our conscience. This is a most precious gift. But can you who are still unbelievers claim the same gift today? You who are yet a sinner, ask yourself this: "Do I have a problem with God? Can I see God's face? What is my relationship with Him? Will I perish?" You probably consider yourself most healthy, so how could you possible perish? But let me remind you that this is only your physical condition. You should instead think of your condition in the sight of God. The Bible lays stress on one sin which all of us must deal with — the matter of our relationship with God; it *must* be corrected.

According to the Bible "there is none righteous, no,

not one" (Rom. 3.10). All of us are sinners because not one of us seeks after God but everyone has turned aside and become altogether unprofitable. The cause for sin lies in our not seeking God nor knowing Him: "all have sinned, and fall short of the glory of God" (Rom. 3.23).

But God has come into this world. The Word has become flesh and has tabernacled among men. God has manifested himself to the world in the person of Jesus of Nazareth. Two thousand years ago God appeared in our midst. He has been preached to us. And the question He will ask you today is this: what is your relationship with this Jesus of Nazareth? Formerly we did not know what kind of god is God; we had only a vague idea of Him. But now, thank God, He has come into the world and has dwelt among us. He is not only God but also Man. He is the Word become flesh. He was crucified to atone for our sins. Today, this Jesus of Nazareth will ask you what your relationship with God is, what you think of Him. And your attitude towards Jesus of Nazareth will be your attitude towards God. For this Jesus of Nazareth is the Word become flesh, He is God clothed with flesh in order to dwell among men.

Do not misunderstand. Hereafter, no one will go to hell because of many different other sins. All who enter hell do so for but one sin—that of not believing in the Son of God: "He that believeth on him is not judged: he that believeth not hath been judged already, because he hath not believed on the name of the only begotten Son of God" (John 3.18). Men are judged not because of killing or committing arson; they are judged for but one reason—they do not believe in the name of the Son of God. Not believing in the name of the Son of God is tantamount to not having a proper relationship with God. The logic of the Bible is that the unbelievers are judged because of their unbelieving. For God looks especially for this sin.

What is your attitude towards Christ today? This is what God will consider, because Christ is the bridge that spans the distance between God and men. He is Man as well as God. Today God dwells among us in Christ. Men's attitude towards Christ is their attitude towards God. Once as I shook hands with a friend he said to me: "Let me take off my gloves first." I replied, "That will be unnecessary, since I shall really be holding your hand and not your gloves." Similarly, Christ is God, except that He is clothed with a human body, just like the hand that has a glove over it. "He that hath seen me," the Lord observed, "hath seen the Father; . . . I am in the Father, and the Father in me" (John 14.9,10). Jesus further explained with these words: "I and the Father are one" (John 10.30).

What the Bible shows us is that after the incarnation of the Lord, the one and only sin which the Holy Spirit convicts people of is that of unbelief: "And he [the Holy Spirit], when he is come, will convict the world in respect of sin, and of righteousness, and of judgment: of sin, because they believe not on me [Christ]" (John 16.8,9). Of sin because they believe not, because they do not have a proper relationship with Christ. The Holy Spirit convicts people not of their killing, perpetrating arson, having pride or jealousy, but of their not having a right relationship with Christ.

Just here I must mention one thing to the believers.

Today much preaching in the church is faulty. People have preached incorrectly not only concerning the Savior, redemption, and salvation, they have also done so with respect to sin. How sin has been inaccurately presented! As if men go to hell for their many sins! Actually there is but one sin which condemns people to hell—that of not having a right relationship with Christ.

How evangelists try to prove men's sinfulness by citing arson, murder, fornication, pride, lying, jealousy, and so on! Now, of course, people should deal with these sins, clear them up with God, and receive forgiveness. Yet even if all these sins are confessed and God's forgiveness is sought, people will not be saved if that one sin is not cleared up. How sad that we pay no attention to the one sin which the Bible emphasizes, the only sin of which the Holy Spirit convicts. There is no doubt that murder, arson, pride, jealousy and so on are truly sins, but the root of all sin is unbelief. The most basic sin, according to the word of God, is unbelief.

Therefore, when we go out to preach the gospel, we do not persuade men to cease killing, burning, despising, or envying, for even if they should stop doing these things they will still perish and not have eternal life. In hell there are countless people like these. In preaching the gospel one thing to insist upon asking people is: is there anything wrong in your relationship with Christ? As long as people do not have a proper relationship with Him, they remain sinners in the sight of God.

This that I have been saying I know whereof I speak.

How Satan attempts to destroy the work of Christ by altering the Biblical emphasis on sin. Today people look at these many fragmentary sins instead of at the root of sin. In so doing they overturn the work of Christ and pursue psychological salvation which is merely moral improvement and change of lifestyle, but not the receiving of life itself. A wrong emphasis on sin will not save souls. Sin is that men do not have the right relationship with God. The younger son was a prodigal because of his controversy with his father. In like manner, if you have a problem with God the Father, this is your sin. I sincerely hope all of us have a proper relationship with God.

"Let all the house of Israel therefore know assuredly, that God hath made him both Lord and Christ, this Jesus whom ye crucified. Now when they heard this, they were pricked in their heart, and said unto Peter and the rest of the apostles, Brethren, what shall we do? And Peter said unto them, Repent ye, and be baptized every one of you in the name of Jesus Christ unto the remission of your sins; and ye shall receive the gift of the Holy Spirit" (Acts 2.36-38). The first work of the Holy Spirit on the day of Pentecost was to prick the heart of those who heard. What had they heard? "God hath made him both Lord and Christ, this Jesus whom ye crucified." This meant that there was something wrong between them and Christ and that they did not have a right relationship with Him. They and God were at odds. God had established Christ as Savior, and they had killed Him. But when they heard this, their hearts were pricked. Not because of their strife with brothers, or their gambling, beating, murder, or arson, but because of their not having a proper relationship with Christ.

"What shall we do?" they asked of Peter and the rest of the apostles. Let us notice Peter's answer here: "Repent ye, and be baptized every one of you in the name of Jesus Christ." He called them first to repent, then to be baptized.

What is repentance? In truth, they did need to repent. Yet let me ask, repent of what? Does repentance point to our former killing but that now we are to kill no more; does it refer to our previous acts of arson but that now we are to do so no more, to our former lying but that now we are to lie no more, to our earlier pride but that now we are to cease being proud anymore? Does repentance refer only to this? No, to repent is to repent of our lack of a proper relationship with God. To repent is to repent of only one thing, and that is, that formerly my relationship with God was wrong, so now I repent. Therefore, we find the apostle Paul declaring both to Jews and to Gentiles "repentance toward God" (Acts 20.21).

To be baptized means to come out of all these things—come out of the world, come out of Adam. Yet how can we come out of the world and of Adam? The only way is to die. And once dead, all is finished. Yesterday I read in the newspaper about a man who asked to have his citizenship revoked. He had to get the permission of the Ministry of the Interior before he could have his status abolished. But when a person is dead, he is freed from all these things pertaining to citizenship—he is freed from national conscription, taxation, the census, and so forth. In like manner, baptism overturns our former position. To be baptized is to acknowledge that when Christ died He took me to the cross with Him and I was thus crucified also. To be crucified is the work of Christ; and to be baptized is to testify to that work. To be buried in baptism is to write the final page in a man's old biography. Death is not the last thing, but burial by means of baptism is: it is the final act: it concludes all that is in Adam.

Please keep ever in mind that the only sin which the Bible stresses is that of not believing Christ. If you have not dealt with this sin by receiving Christ as your Savior, you are doomed. With *this* sin dealt with, however, all the other fragmentary sins can easily be resolved. Without having this sin dealt with, and even if all the other sins are solved, you will still go to hell. May God give us all a proper relationship with Christ. May He constrain us to deal properly with this one sin. We thank God, for His view of sin is quite different from ours. May we, like Him, also have the right emphasis concerning sin.

3 | Forgiveness and Confession

To forgive is God's heart desire. He loves men and delights in forgiving their sins. Ever since man fell, God has provided ways to atone for sins.

In the Old Testament time, God used bullocks and sheep to atone for men's sins. In the New Testament period, He appoints the Lord Jesus—the Lamb of God—as the sin-offering, who then offered himself once for all to obtain eternal redemption for men. In God's view, the shed blood of the Lord Jesus on the cross has completely solved the sin problem of the world. But from humanity's standpoint man still needs to add one ingredient—faith. Whoever believes that the blood of the Lord Jesus was shed for his sins, that one is redeemed and the person's trespasses are forgiven. Anyone who disbelieves will perish and go to hell. But so far as atonement is concerned, the work is already done. It is of God, originated by God, and is what God wants to do. He does it by sacrificing His only begotten Son, a tremendous price that God has paid. Hence, there is absolutely no question that God wants to forgive sins and to provide for men the means of atonement. Are there any sinners who are still afraid that their sins cannot be forgiven? God wants to forgive such people. He delights in forgiving them, and He has already paid a great price to forgive them.

God Is Able to Forgive All Sins

Whenever a *sinner* believes that the Lord Jesus shed His blood on the cross for his sins, that person's sins shall be forgiven at that very moment. If a *believer* is overtaken in any trespass and sins, he will be forgiven if he honestly repents and confesses his sin before God (1 John 1.9). For the blood price the Lord Jesus has paid is great enough to forgive all sins and to cleanse all unrighteousness. So the way of forgiveness is open to saints as well as sinners.

God Forgives Forever

On one occasion the Lord Jesus said to Peter that he must forgive seventy times seven, which means he must keep on forgiving and forever forgiving as long as his brother is willing to repent. Since the blessed Lord taught *Peter* such gracious words, would He not *himself* put His own words into practice? Surely God will forgive all who are sorry for their sins and who truly repent. He will forgive them forever.

God's Forgiveness Leaves No Mark

Many people think that sinning is like making an

error in writing, and forgiveness is like erasing that error which will nevertheless leave an indelible mark. They do not realize that this is absolutely untrue in God's forgiveness. The blood of the Lord Jesus cleanses men's sins. What is cleansing? Cleansing is a process so perfect that it leaves no spot. Our sins are so washed away as though we had never sinned and as though we were as holy as Christ himself: "Come now, and let us reason together, saith Jehovah: though your sins be as scarlet, they shall be as white as snow; though they be red like crimson, they shall be as wool" (Is. 1.18). Look how white snow and wool are, for there is not one speck of red. Accordingly, when God washes away sins, He leaves no mark behind but cleanses purely and perfectly.

God's Heart to Forgive Surpasses Our Heart for Forgiveness

What the father in Luke 15 did to the prodigal son enables us to know the forgiving heart of our heavenly Father toward sinners. While the prodigal son was yet on the way home, his father saw him afar off and ran to meet him. The old man did not stroll slowly; he *ran*. His heart was so eager after his son that walking was too slow for him. His legs *had* to move quickly. Today God's legs of forgiveness also run after every repentant sinner. How He *longs* to forgive man's sins as rapidly as possible. Did the prodigal run towards his father? No, he did not. Judging from the movements of them both, we can readily see that the father's heart of forgiving surpasses the son's heart for forgiveness. If we continue observing how the father fell on his neck and kissed him repeatedly, we shall understand what pleasure God the Father himself takes in a repentant sinner. Though the son hated what he had done and felt guilty towards heaven and his father, and continued confessing his sins to the father, the latter, out of intense love for his son, was impatient to allow his son to finish his confession, and therefore commanded instead that the servants fetch the best robe and put a ring and shoes on the prodigal son (please note that there were less words of confession recorded in verse 21 than in verses 18 and 19 because the father broke in).

How precious to know that our heavenly Father's love to forgive exceeds our heart for forgiveness. He does not wait for us to cry three days and three nights, confessing over and over again before He will forgive. Frequently we cry and cry, confess and confess, beat ourselves black and blue—in order to be forgiven. How we misconstrue God's heart, and in actuality we wound His heart. Let us realize that he loves those whom He has bought with a price far more than we could ever love ourselves. How He longs to forgive us, indeed He "runs" to forgive us. And before we can even finish our confession, He has already forgiven us!

How often when your loved one in the family sins against you, you are anxious to forgive. You will immediately forgive him if he is willing merely to apologize. Truly, where there is love, there is the forgiving heart. If this is factual among men, how much more this is the case with the heavenly Father, who is full of mercy and compassion to eternally and completely forgive the sins of men.

God Cannot But Forgive

God sent the Lord Jesus to the earth to shed his blood on the cross for the sins of the world that the problem of sin might be resolved. All this speaks of the loving heart of God. But after the Lord Jesus had shed His blood, God himself bore witness to Him, saying that all who believe shall have their sins forgiven — that all who confess shall have their unrighteousness cleansed. Have faith if you are a sinner, confess if you are a believer, and God cannot but forgive your sins. Otherwise, God would be unfaithful and unrighteous. Let me reverently ask how the holy God could ever be unfaithful and unrighteous? Oh, this fact of sins forgiven is something guaranteed! Let us rejoice in God, for sin shall not reign over us. We are delivered from sin and we are forgiven.

God's Grace of Forgiveness Is to Lead Us to Repentance

God's truth has two sides. What has already been mentioned stresses the side of grace which is true and guaranteed. As long as a person is kept in the grace of God, he has nothing to fear regarding the matter of "sins forgiven." Even so, if anyone should think that he can *waste* the grace of God — that is to say, "Shall we continue in sin, that grace may abound?" (Rom. 6.1) — let him read the following sobering words: "Behold then the goodness and severity of God: toward them that fell, severity; but toward thee, God's goodness, if thou continue in his goodness: otherwise thou also shalt be cut off" (Rom. 11.22).

Some have dared to say: "I sin daily by hiding under the precious blood;" or, "I sin in the daytime and confess before God in the evening to have my sins forgiven. I go on sinning the next day, and keep on confessing the next evening for forgiveness. Since the Lord Jesus taught Peter to forgive seventy times seven, surely He will forgive me. And then, too, there are the words in 1 John 1.9 that, God being faithful and righteous, He cannot but forgive my sins which I confess, for Christ has already died on the cross for me."

Thou fool, do you not know that *the grace of God is to lead you to repentance* (see Rom. 2.4) and not to encourage you to sin? If you think you can waste the precious blood, it shows that the precious blood has never washed away your so-called "confessed" sins.

The Condition for a Christian to Be Forgiven

Let us answer this question with the word of God: "if we walk in the light, as he is in the light, we have fellowship one with another, and the blood of Jesus his Son cleanseth us from all sin" (1 John 1.7).

From this verse we learn that there is one condition and two consequences. From the one condition there flows two consequences without failure. What is the condition here? "If we walk in the light as he [God] is in the light." This means that if we Christians walk in the light, we are not walking in darkness, and therefore we shall have works of light and not deeds of darkness. What kind of light is this? Or what degree of light is it? The light here corresponds to the words, "as he [God] is in the light"; and according to verse 5, "God is light, and in him is no darkness at all" (note that all other lights are mixed up with darkness).

Thus walking in God's light will bring two consequences. *First,* "we have fellowship one with another"—that is to say, we have fellowship with brothers and sisters in the Lord. With the above condition fulfilled we can fellowship with one another. If there is no fellowship it must be due to the condition unfulfilled. Then, the *second* consequence is, "and the blood of Jesus his Son cleanseth us from all sin." This means that having walked in the light we find the precious blood being effective in cleansing all our sins. So that it is clear to us that "fellowship one with another" and "the blood cleanses us from all our sin" flow out of the condition, "if we walk in the light." If a Christian does not walk in the light, he will lose the benefit of "fellowshiping one with another" as well as that of "the blood cleansing from all sin." And to reverse it, we may say that in order to have fellowship and cleansing one must walk in the light; otherwise, there will be neither fellowship nor cleansing.

The first consequence—fellowship—is visible. It can be experienced on earth and is experienced in the sight of men. The second consequence—the cleansing—is invisible, yet it is a fact in heaven before God. As the visible is factual on earth, so the invisible is factual in heaven. As it is true before men, so it is true before God. For this reason, a Christian who sins is not able to fellowship freely with other Christians on earth; rather, he will attempt to avoid them.

Let me warn you most solemnly that if you sin and walk in darkness, you will not only lose fellowship with other believers but will also miss the effectual cleansing of your sins by the precious blood before God. As you lose the first consequence for not walking in the light, so you will forfeit the second consequence also. You may confess your sins with your mouth, yet you will not be cleansed by the precious blood. This is not, however, because the precious blood has lost its cleansing power, but because your situation of not walking in the light does not fulfill the condition for cleansing. For the condition for cleansing is to *"walk in the light,"* but you continue to sin and to walk in darkness; therefore the precious blood will not cleanse you. The precious blood will only cleanse the sin of those who walk in the light.

Consequently, do not deceive yourselves. If you sin and fall and lose the fellowship which is visible on earth, I fear you will also miss the cleansing of the precious blood which is invisible in heaven. Let me warn you most earnestly that if you refuse to deal with your sin with a truly sorrowful and repentant heart, you will have to stand before the judgment seat of Christ to settle your account. Hence, a confession of sin from the mouth without a corresponding deed of "walking in the light" and a heart truly sorrowful and repentant (Ps. 51.17) will not result in cleansing.

What I would especially emphasize is this one condition of *"walking in the light,"* because this condition is often neglected by those who have wasted the precious blood (in actuality the precious blood can never be wasted by them)—though it is their only remedy. This is why I want to stress this point. According to the Bible, for a believer to receive forgiveness after having sinned, at least the following three conditions must be present: (1) a broken and contrite heart (Ps. 51.17); (2) a confession of our sins (1 John 1.9); and (3) a walking in the light (1 John 1.7). If anyone should assume that he can sin daily by hiding under the precious blood or that he can sin in the day and confess at night, let me emphatically declare that there is no such thing. God will not be mocked. Whenever one walks in darkness, then he is not cleansed by the precious blood, for the blood cannot serve as one's shelter or refuge. If a person wishes to be cleansed by the precious blood, he must first walk in the light and purpose to sin no more.

True confession must be in line with Paul's observation when he wrote to the previously "puffed up" and "glorying" Corinthian believers (1 Cor. 5.2,6) that "ye were made sorry unto repentance; for ye were made sorry after a godly sort, . . . for godly sorrow worketh repentance unto salvation, a repentance which bringeth no regret" (2 Cor. 7.9b,10a). Furthermore, according to the apostle Paul, such genuine repentance is characterized by the following seven traits: (1) earnest care, (2) the clearing of oneself, (3) indignation, (4) fear, (5) longing, (6) zeal, and (7) avenging (see 2 Cor. 7.11). He who exhibits these seven traits is truly confessing his sin. Otherwise, one's "confession" is merely of the lips, not of the heart. The mouth may confess the sin, but the heart does not hate it. If so, then let me repeat that the precious blood is not operative in such a person.

Some keep on sinning because they have acquired a formula for forgiveness of sin. He knows by heart

1 John 1.9 that "if we confess our sins, he is faithful and righteous to forgive us our sins, and to cleanse us from all unrighteousness." He figures that since the Lord Jesus has shed His precious blood for him, surely this precious blood is able to cleanse his sins. At the same time, God, being faithful and righteous, will without fail forgive all his sins and cleanse him from all unrighteousness if he but confesses his sins. Having obtained this "magic charm," as it were, he can afford to be less careful, for has he not achieved the way of forgiveness? Surely he can sin a little, if only he confesses his sin as well. Yet how perilous is the position of such a person!

Once I heard of a brother A who opened a private letter of a brother B. And after he looked into it, A confessed to B on this wise: "It is not right, I know, to open and read another person's letter, but I knew you would forgive me, so I went ahead to open and read it." Now this illustrates how one deliberately sins upon his knowing the way of forgiveness. Yet this is a falling into the snare of the devil. Such a person has stumbled upon a hidden rock along the spiritual pathway. It is a most perilous path to follow. May all who only know the *formula* of forgiveness but who do not know as well the *condition* of "walking in the light" fear and tremble lest they sin against God. Let me reiterate that the goodness and grace of God should lead us to repentance (Rom. 2.4), not encourage us to sin!

Four Kinds of Heart Condition in Confession

When people realize they have sinned and have then

confessed either to God or to men, their heart conditions may be quite different from each other. From my personal observation, I have detected at least four different conditions of the heart in people. Let us examine each of these in some detail.

(1) *An uneasiness in one's own conscience.* After a person has sinned, his conscience becomes uneasy and accuses him. By confessing his sin, his conscience returns to peace and no longer accuses him. It is permissible to confess sin due to the accusation of one's conscience. But if one confesses only for the sake of the peace of one's conscience—for the sake of stopping its accusing voice—yet without seeing a deeper reason for confession (this deeper reason being to cultivate a hatefulness of the sin itself), such confession is but a bribing of the conscience. For conscience is the organ in us which tells us of our actual condition. It accuses because sin is hateful. It persists in raising its voice against sin. Now you are tired of its accusation and conceive of a way to stop its accusation, but you fail to hate the sin that the conscience hates. What you pay attention to is the accusing conscience and not the cause of its accusation, which is sin. You do not hate sin, you are merely uneasy over the accusation of the conscience. You do not deal with the root of the matter—sin; instead, you deal with the accusation which comes out of the root—that is to say, the conscience. With the result that you use the method of confession to bribe your conscience. But God demands much more than that.

(2) *A fear of an accusation by the other person's conscience.* Sometimes you offend a person and regret

what you did. Meanwhile you are afraid this other person will hate you and accuse you of being wrong. In order to appease his conscience and restore peace, you find an opportunity to confess to him. You figure that if he forgives you, you will be reconciled to him. He will no longer hate you and his conscience will not accuse you anymore. And if he will *not* forgive you, then this becomes *his* problem before God (and not yours any longer) and it will be to his disadvantage ("if ye forgive not men their trespasses, neither will your Father forgive your trespasses" [Matthew 6.15]). Such a mental attitude is not much different from the first heart condition described above because what it deals with is not sin itself, but the other person's conscience. There is nothing wrong in our being reconciled with other people, but a failure to hate the sin itself is not the kind of heart condition which God requires in our dealing with sin.

If your confession only flows out from the above two heart conditions, the inevitable result will be an easiness to sin and an easiness to confess. You do not sense in your heart that each time you sin against men you sin against God. You do not feel the absolute necessity of the precious blood. You are only conscious of your relationship with man. As long as you are reconciled with him you reckon it is satisfactory enough. Yet you do not see the hatefulness of sin, nor do you realize the seriousness of confession. Moreover, you will not have a truly broken and contrite heart, and you do not find it an embarrassing thing to confess your sin. To sum up, you look lightly upon sin, and consequently you can easily sin again. You may sometimes even commit *the same sin* as you are in the process of confessing it. May God give all of us grace that we may see sin as *He* sees it.

(3) *A fear of future punishment.* Someone may recall the solemn words of 2 Corinthians 5.10 that "we must all be made manifest before the judgment-seat of Christ; that each one may receive the things done in the body, according to what he hath done, whether it be good or bad." He knows of the awaiting judgment before the judgment-seat of Christ. Not only his works will be judged, his life will be judged also. Whatever has not been judged by conscience under the illumination of the Holy Spirit and has not been cleansed by the precious blood will be judged by the Lord in the days to come. Hence he harbors fear in his heart. Since today's sins will be judged in the future anyway, it is most profitable to clear them up now than to be judged for them later.

Now it is not wrong for you to confess with this kind of heart condition; as a matter of fact, this is better than the above two conditions, since with respect to just the first two, you are only related to men, but with respect to this third heart condition you are at least related to God. You confess your sins out of a fear of God. Obviously, your confession has two sides: on the one hand, you confess to God; on the other hand, you also confess to men (if you have sinned against them). And upon confessing, you maintain a conscience without offense both towards God and towards men. This is commendable, but it is still not the highest kind of heart condition in confession.

(4) *A seeing the uncleanness of sin.* This is the kind of heart condition God truly wants. And why? Because God has put His own life in us, and with this life, we have a most holy nature (as holy a nature as God has). Sin is most unclean in the sight of God, and it is absolutely incompatible to His holy nature. God gives His holy life to us that we may hate sin as He hates it. If we allow this holy life to grow in us, we will recognize the uncleanliness of sin. We will cry out as did Madame Guyon, when she declared: "I would rather go to hell than to want to sin." The life of God in us is to manifest Christ. The more manifested is the nature of Christ, the more hateful to us will sin appear, and the farther apart from sin we shall become (see Heb. 7.26). Let us look at sin as we do leprosy: the farther away we are from it the more comfortable we become! All who have such an understanding of sin as this will not sin easily. If confession is done with such a heart condition as this fourth kind, that person will live a godly and holy life before God.

How to Cultivate the Right Knowledge of Sin

How can we develop a right knowledge of sin? This requires the enlightenment of the Holy Spirit and our obedience to the light. We must reject all sins which have been exposed by light. The Holy Spirit who moves in our spirit will reveal to us the character of all sins. He will also cause our renewed mind to know how most unclean sin is as well as cause our conscience to rise up and condemn sin as sin. Meanwhile, our new life — the life of Christ — naturally hates sin, since such an aversion to sin is a characteristic of God's very nature (see 2 Peter 1.4). Let me simply point out that the Holy Spirit reveals the reality of sin by the light of life,* and according to the nature of God's life in us we obey the light and hate the sin which is revealed by the light.

Hence the more we obey the light, the brighter will the light shine within us, the dirtier will the sin be manifested, and the stronger will be the animosity of our hearts toward sin. It is similar to the way minute particles of dust which float in the air and which are not usually visible become visible under the bright sunlight. Hence one who abides in God's strong light will condemn as sin those things which others might not ever consider to be sin. Madame Guyon, for example, repented of her former deeds of giving alms and asked for the cleansing of the precious blood when, under the light of God, she finally perceived that her former good deeds had been done out of her own good and not out of the life of God. She therefore realized that they needed cleansing by the blood. Like Madame Guyon, a person will become increasingly more sensitive to sin, and one's practical holiness will also be greatly increased.

We may say that just as the nature of one who belongs to Adam (that is, the nature of an unregenerated person) *inclines toward* sin, so the nature of God in one who belongs to Christ *abhors and is repelled*

---

*Let us take note of the words found in John 1.4 ("the life was the light of men"). The life of Christ in men is the light of men. It is not something which is outwardly visible, and therefore all who look for outside light are exposed to the danger of deception. —*Author* by sin. Aversion toward sin is the natural expression of God's nature in men. Such kind of heart condition is of God and well-pleasing to God.

By our analyzing these four kinds of heart condition, I believe we can now easily conclude that the first three are centered upon self and are directly related to self-interest, whereas only the last one is centered upon God and is of God. And those with this fourth kind of heart truly stand on God's side.

Confession Must Be Made to God First

Concerning this matter of confessing sin, there is a bad tendency among Christians to incline gradually more and more to having dealings with men rather than having dealings with God. There are even Christians who do not mention the precious blood at all. They only seek for the peace of conscience with each other, putting God aside completely. Such a situation is most dreadful, since it will end up in their losing the fear of God. Let me most emphatically state: the notion of *confession without the need of the precious blood must incontrovertibly emanate from hell.* Let us ever keep in mind that in our committing each sin *God*, not *man*, is the first one who is being offended. God, not man, is the one who is most frequently being sinned against. (It is not unlike the fact that when you break a piece of furniture in someone's house, the *first* you offend is the *owner* of the house, not the *thing* belonging to the owner.)

Recall how David confessed in Psalm 51.4, "Against thee, thee only, have I sinned." He did not say here that he had sinned against Uriah or against Bathsheba (though obviously David *had* sinned against them as well). In contrast to David's heart, we find that Judas the betrayer of the Lord Jesus confessed his sin to men and returned the money; but though Judas cleared up the matter with men, he nevertheless remained a son of perdition. By my saying these things I do not wish to be misunderstood as meaning that we should not confess to one another, because confessing to one another is something right and Biblical for us to do (see James 5.16). I only stress that it is more important to deal with God than with men. *We should never reverse the order.* We must not put aside God and the precious blood. It is essential to confess our sins before God, and it is also essential that we not neglect clearing up matters with men. May God have mercy upon us.

4 | David and Mephibosheth

Now Jonathan, Saul's son, had a son that was lame of his feet. He was five years old when the tidings came of Saul and Jonathan out of Jezreel; and his nurse took him up, and fled: and it came to pass, as she made haste to flee, that he fell, and became lame. And his name was Mephibosheth. (2 Sam. 4.4)

And David said, Is there yet any that is left of the house of Saul, that I may show him kindness for Jonathan's sake? And there was of the house of Saul a servant whose name was Ziba, and they called him unto David; and the king said unto him, Art thou Ziba? And he said, Thy servant is he. And the king said, Is there not yet any of the house of Saul, that I may show the kindness of God unto him? And Ziba said unto the king, Jonathan hath yet a son, who is lame of his feet. And the king said unto him, Where is he? And Ziba said unto the king, Behold, he is in the house of Machir the son of Ammiel, in Lodebar. Then king David sent, and fetched him out of the house of Machir the son of Ammiel, from

Lodebar. And Mephibosheth, the son of Jonathan, the
son of Saul, came unto David, and fell on his face, and
did obeisance. And David said, Mephibosheth. And he
answered, Behold, thy servant! And David said unto him,
Fear not; for I will surely show thee kindness for Jonathan
thy father's sake, and will restore thee all the land of Saul
thy father; and thou shalt eat bread at my table continually. And he did obeisance, and said, What is thy servant,
that thou shouldest look upon such a dead dog as I am?
Then the king called to Ziba, Saul's servant, and said unto
him, All that pertained to Saul and to all his house have
I given unto thy master's son. And thou shalt till the land
for him, thou, and thy sons, and thy servants; and thou
shalt bring in the fruits, that thy master's son may have
bread to eat: but Mephibosheth thy master's son shall eat
bread alway at my table. Now Ziba had fifteen sons and
twenty servants. Then said Ziba unto the king, According
to all that my lord the king commandeth his servant, so
shall thy servant do. As for Mephibosheth, said the king,
he shall eat at my table, as one of the king's sons. And
Mephibosheth had a young son, whose name was Mica.
And all that dwelt in the house of Ziba were servants unto Mephibosheth. So Mephibosheth dwelt in Jerusalem;
for he did eat continually at the king's table. And he was
lame in both his feet. (2 Sam. 9.1-13)

And when David was a little past the top of the ascent, behold, Ziba the servant of Mephibosheth met him,
with a couple of asses saddled, and upon them two hundred loaves of bread, and a hundred clusters of raisins,
and a hundred of summer fruits, and a bottle of wine.
And the king said unto Ziba, What meanest thou by these?
And Ziba said, The asses are for the king's household to

ride on; and the bread and summer fruit for the young men to eat; and the wine, that such as are faint in the wilderness may drink. And the king said, And where is thy master's son? And Ziba said unto the king, Behold, he abideth at Jerusalem; for he said, Today will the house of Israel restore me the kingdom of my father. Then said the king to Ziba, Behold, thine is all that pertaineth unto Mephibosheth. And Ziba said, I do obeisance; let me find favor in thy sight, my lord, O king. (2 Sam. 16.1-4)

And Mephibosheth the son of Saul came down to meet the king; and he had neither dressed his feet, nor trimmed his beard, nor washed his clothes, from the day the king departed until the day he came home in peace. And it came to pass, when he was come to Jerusalem to meet the king, that the king said unto him, Wherefore wentest not thou with me, Mephibosheth? And he answered, My lord, O king, my servant deceived me: for thy servant said, I will saddle me an ass, that I may ride thereon, and go with the king; because thy servant is lame. And he hath slandered thy servant unto my lord the king; but my lord the king is as an angel of God: do therefore what is good in thine eyes. For all my father's house were but dead men before my lord the king; yet didst thou set thy servant among them that did eat at thine own table. What right therefore have I yet that I should cry any more unto the king? And the king said unto him, Why speakest thou any more of thy matters? I say, Thou and Ziba divide the land. And Mephibosheth said unto the king, Yea, let him take all, forasmuch as my lord the king is come in peace unto his own house. (2 Sam. 19.24-30)

But the king spared Mephibosheth, the son of Jonathan the son of Saul, because of Jehovah's oath that

was between them, between David and Jonathan the son
of Saul. (2 Sam. 21.7)

Let us observe a marvelous scene in the Old Testament: a lame child sat at the king's table. As a matter
of fact, the New Testament is full of marvelous things
too — such as a harlot being saved, a robber being saved,
a publican being saved, and a Pharisee being saved.
Here, however, we see that a lame child was saved.

Whenever we who have read the Scriptures think
of friendship, we will most likely mention David and
Jonathan. Even in world literature, the story of David
and Jonathan is used as an illustration of friendly love.
Yet the emphasis which I would like us to focus on in
this story of the lame child in 2 Samuel is on how David
treated Mephibosheth the son of Jonathan with kindness and not on how Mephibosheth expressed his
gratitude to David.

Mephibosheth Was Lame (4.4)

"Now Jonathan, Saul's son, had a son that was lame
of his feet. He was five years old when the tidings came
of Saul and Jonathan out of Jezreel; and his nurse took
him up, and fled: and it came to pass, as she made haste
to flee, that he fell, and became lame. And his name
was Mephibosheth." (4.4)

One fact to be recalled is that Saul, the grandfather
of Mephibosheth, had been an enemy of David. How
he had frequently persecuted David, wishing to put him
to death. But now both Saul and Jonathan had been
killed in warfare. And Mephibosheth's nurse had taken

up the child and fled. This was the only child left to his grandfather and his father. If he had not fled with his nurse, Mephibosheth might have been killed later on by David. But in the haste to flee, the child had fallen to the ground and had thus become lame. Is not this entire situation a picture of every sinner's attitude towards God? Allow me to explain.

Oh, how man misunderstands God! Because man has evil thoughts about God, he believes God thinks evilly of him too. Because he hates God, he surmises that God also hates him. He knows he has sinned, therefore he concludes that God hates him. Mephibosheth may have reflected that David must hate him because his grandfather Saul had been David's arch enemy. David could not possibly love him since he himself had no affection for David. In like manner do we think about God. Would God ever love us since we have no affection for Him? Would God ever love us since we hate Him? Permit me to say that God's attitude is absolutely opposite to yours. Mephibosheth had not the slightest idea of receiving grace, yet he received abundant grace. And so will God treat us with grace too.

David Dealt Kindly with Mephibosheth (9.1-13)

"And David said, Is there yet any that is left of the house of Saul, that I may show him kindness for Jonathan's sake?" (v.1)

Today God is continually asking if there is any left of Adam towards whom He can show kindness. David expressed kindness to Mephibosheth for the sake of

Jonathan. And God shows kindness to sinners for the sake of His Son Christ Jesus. How men have erred in thinking that God hates them. They imagine they have to do much good in order to turn God's face towards them, to appease His anger, and for Him to be pleased with them. But Mephibosheth had no position whatsoever before David. Nor did David know him, for he only knew Jonathan, Mephibosheth's father. Yet for Jonathan's sake, he would show kindness to his son.

Now it was not due to any good which Mephibosheth did to earn David's favor. Mephibosheth received grace not because of himself but because of a third person. So is it with a sinner before God. Some may fancy they have to do something good first before they can court God's pleasure; but the Bible tells us God loves us *without any cause*. We have no position before Him and we should not receive His care; nevertheless we too have a Jonathan, even Jesus Christ, and for His sake God extends kindness to us. We are saved because before God there is the Lord Jesus Christ. With Him we can come before the presence of God.

In former days at the university, a student had been required to take two years of preparatory studies before he could take the main courses; and at some medical colleges three years of preparatory courses had been required. Let me tell you, however, that no one needs to take any preparatory courses for his salvation. How many conceive the idea that they have to prepare a little to restore God's heart. Not so! We do not need to do anything to court His pleasure. Nowhere in the Scriptures is it said that God wants to be reconciled to us; it says instead that *we* are to be reconciled to God! God loved us, so He gave His Son to us. He did not give His Son to us in order that He might love us. Some people speculate that fortunately for us the Lord Jesus has died so that God could love us. Not at all, God first loved us, and therefore He gave His Son to us.

"And the king said, Is there not yet any of the house of Saul, that I may show the kindness of God unto him? And Ziba said unto the king, Jonathan hath yet a son, who is lame of his feet. And the king said unto him, Where is he? And Ziba said unto the king, Behold, he is in the house of Machir the son of Ammiel, in Lodebar" (vv.3,4). "Lodebar" in Hebrew means "no pasture." The world today is like Lodebar. Lodebar could never make people full nor quench their thirst. It could not satisfy men's hearts. Let us recognize the fact that we human beings were created for God, and not for ourselves. Those who have not returned to God will never be satisfied.

You may have dreamed of a beautiful and restful future. But as time goes on, what the world seems to promise cannot be cashed in. It will disappoint you time and again until you finally realize what you have is but a dream, a mirage, a land of no pasture. Do understand that a life without God is an unsatisfied life. A life outside of God is never fulfilling. Mephibosheth away from David lived in a land without pasture; even so, a sinner away from God also lives in a land of no pasture.

What did David do when he heard that Mephibosheth lived in a land of no pasture? Praise and thank God, that "king David sent, and fetched him out of the house of Machir the son of Ammiel, from Lodebar" (v.5). Romans 3.11 declares that "there is none that seeketh after God"; and Luke 19.10 records the fact that "the Son of man came to seek and to save that which was lost." Some people might conclude that at least we "no good people" would surely seek after God, that surely the fallen would search for Him. Yet the fact of the matter is that if God were to wait for us to find him, we would never be saved because we would not and do not seek after Him. Mephibosheth did not have the courage to seek after David, since his grandfather had been David's enemy; nor had he the strength to make the search because he was lame in his two feet. It was not Mephibosheth who sought after David, it was David who sent and fetched Mephibosheth. Just so with us as unbelievers; it is not that *we* seek after God, but that *God* sent His Son to seek us out and to bring us back to himself.

The Bible makes clear that it is *God* who wants you, it is *God* who calls you, it is *God* who sends people to tell you He wants you. "Say not in thy heart, Who shall ascend into heaven? (that is, to bring Christ down): or, Who shall descend into the abyss? (that is, to bring Christ up from the dead)" (Rom. 10.6,7). Here we are told that no one can go up to heaven to ask the Lord to come and die for him, nor is there anyone who can go down to hell to bring Christ up from the dead. This is immediately followed by the statement: "The word is nigh thee, in thy mouth, and in thy heart: . . . because if thou shalt confess with thy mouth Jesus as Lord, and shalt believe in thy heart that God raised him from the dead, thou shalt be saved" (10.8,9). Like Mephibosheth, no one needs to do or spend anything, because the king himself had sent and fetched for Mephibosheth. And so too with the Lord and sinners. If anyone is still un-saved today, it is not because God does not save him, but because he resists His grace.

What did David say to Mephibosheth after sending for him? "And Mephibosheth, the son of Jonathan, the son of Saul, came unto David, and fell on his face, and did obeisance. And David said, *Mephibosheth*. And he answered, Behold, thy servant!" (v.6) What a sweet sound to the ear! "Mephibosheth." When David saw Jonathan's son, he did not say to him, "Who are you?" Neither did he say to him, "Mephibosheth, the son of Jonathan, the son of Saul"; nor did he say, "Mephibosheth, so you are here." He merely said, "Mephibosheth." Just imagine, if you can, how David must have felt in his heart. With what kind of tone did he utter that name? For behind this word was a stirred-up heart which represents the heart of God towards you and me. To say "Mephibosheth" expresses the fact that God does not hate you and me, but rather that He wants us and loves us. Each time our name is called without any additional word, it carries a deep meaning within it which heaven alone can totally appreciate.

I have mentioned on other occasions the story of how Mary Magdalene mistook the Lord to be a gardener. The Lord did not answer with, "I am not a gardener"; or with, "I have not taken His body away"; or with, "Woman, how could you possibly carry the body?" He merely said, "Mary!" As she heard this most familiar sound, she instantly responded with "Rabboni!" And here we see David beholding the grandson of his archenemy, and he simply said, "Mephibosheth." This reflects the fact that in David's heart there was no trace of animosity but only fullness of compassion.

Unfortunately, Mephibosheth did not know David's heart. When he came into the presence of the king, his heart must have been beating hard because he was to meet the ruler of Judah who might have him killed. And after he saw David and heard him call "Mephibosheth," he should have understood that the king had no ill will towards him but only tender affection. Nevertheless, his fear was so deep that he responded with, "Behold, thy servant." Perhaps he figured that if he, a grandson of the former king, would humble himself to be a slave, he might please David's heart and be spared from being killed. Yet let us all be assured of the fact that no one can possibly earn God's pleasure by his works as a servant.

As though to demonstrate the heart of God, David said to Mephibosheth, "Fear not; for I will surely show thee kindness for Jonathan thy father's sake, and will restore thee all the land of Saul thy father; and thou shalt eat bread at my table continually" (v.7). By this we see that all is well. I wonder who among us truly knows that God loves him? Some may have worked for the Lord many years but still do not know that He loves them. If we truly know that God loves us, our lives will undergo a tremendous change.

During the nineteenth century, there lived in America a man eminent in literature. He was the editor of a well-known newspaper, but he was also very much against Christianity. One day he heard the preaching of D. L. Moody and was saved. Many American newspapers printed the story of his conversion. On one occasion, J. Wilbur Chapman happened to be in a certain city and stayed in a hotel room next door to this very man. Having known him before, Mr. Chapman asked if the story about his conversion were true. Upon which he replied: "I indeed repented and believed in the Lord Jesus after hearing Moody's preaching. However, I need to add that when I was eighteen, I had already come to know the Lord God. I myself had been a prodigal son in my earlier youth. Unaccustomed to being shut in the house, I left home for a number of years when I was only twelve years old. But in my adolescence, I became seriously ill. I spent all my money, and in extremity I despondently returned home.

"My father treated me well, yet I regretted I had come home. This was because my father was old, his hair was hoary, and he had contracted a certain disease. Every day he forced himself despite his ill-health to go out to work in order to exchange his labor for some bread to feed us. But the income was so little that it was not enough to feed three people. I was truly sorry that I had come home. I could not bear anymore to eat the bread which was being earned at the expense of my father's blood.

"As my strength regained itself a little, I immediately notified my father that I was leaving. Never in my life had I seen such sadness. He said to me, 'You are not well yet; why must you leave? As long as this home has a piece of bread, there is always your share: as long as there is a piece of tile on the roof, there is your share underneath it. Why must you go?' But I was determined to leave home. So he said to me, 'My child, let me tell you, never in my life have I thought of getting rich, but today because of you I wish that I *were* rich, that I might have more money to keep you from wandering away from home. We may get some help yet, so why must you go?' However, I could not but go because I could not bear anymore to eat the bread which was earned at the cost of my father's blood. Finally, my father said, 'Child, may God bless you! I may not see you today, but I hope to see you in heaven!'

"In sending me away, he walked with me for half a mile without saying anything, and neither did I utter any word. After a mile, he was too tired to walk farther. So at that point he said goodbye to me. On that day, I realized how hard it was to leave home! After having taken two steps, he turned and called me. With tears in his eyes, he took out of his pocket a half dollar and gave it to me. He said, 'This is for you.' I knew what this half dollar meant. I knew that all my father had in the world was bound up in this half dollar. For the first time I realized how my father loved me! I stood there watching my father going home. Although the day was raining and the air was rather chilly, I felt great warmth in my heart. I sang all the way afterwards, My father loves me!

"From that day onward, I was no longer to be prodigal. I determined first of all to lessen the burden on my father: the very first dollar I was to earn would be sent to him because he loved me. Thereafter I was a changed person. This did not mean that my father had not loved me before; it simply meant that at the time of my utmost destitution I realized how he loved me. So one day I heard Mr. Moody preach, saying: 'Many people talk about the father's prodigal son in Luke 15, but I will talk today about the prodigal's father.' And

I saw that that father was the same as my own father, and therefore I believed and received Jesus as my Savior."

Let me observe that I have known this God for quite a number of years now. I know indeed what His heart is like. Do not conceive the thought of doing anything to restore His heart's pleasure towards you. Let me unequivocally declare that He loves you and wills that you be saved. He has no need for you to regain His heart. Many will say God has not told them He loves them; but please look at the cross, and then you will know that He has loved you. The death penalty of the cross is yours, but for the sake of love, God has caused the Lord Jesus to die in your place.

What is love? Love is not mere word. As a matter of fact, the deepest love is unspeakable. Recall how the prodigal son had prepared to say to his father, "Father, I have sinned against heaven, and in thy sight: I am no more worthy to be called thy son: make me as one of thy hired servants" (Luke 15.18,19). But while he was yet afar off, his father saw him and was deeply moved with compassion, and ran, and fell on his neck, and kissed him. "Ran" is the word used in the story, and it reflects how the father's heart greatly desired to shorten the distance of sin. When his father kissed him, the prodigal came to know his father's heart. Yet his father had not said, "I love you;" instead, his kiss told the prodigal of the father's heart. He was not able to finish his preconceived thought of saying, "Make me as one of thy servants," for his father's heart had told him by this kiss that his father indeed loved him.

Please do not misunderstand God's heart. Come to

the foot of the cross. Jesus has died for you; and by this is revealed to you God's heart towards you. In seeing the blood of the Lord Jesus, you know what love God has for you.

"Then the king called to Ziba, Saul's servant, and said unto him, All that pertained to Saul and to all his house have I given unto my master's son. And thou shalt till the land for him, thou, and thy sons, and thy servants; and thou shalt bring in the fruits, that thy master's son may have bread to eat: but Mephibosheth thy master's son shall eat bread alway at my table. . . . As for Mephibosheth, said the king, he shall eat at my table, as one of the king's sons" (vv.9-11). How marvelous that there is not one condition nor any command but all is promise. Here nothing is said as to what one must do and how much. It is all being given; and this is grace. If we understand God's love, we cannot but believe in Him.

Man's Repentance

Probably some may ask that if a sinner will be saved merely by believing in God, is there any need for repentance? Please do not reverse the order found in the Bible. Many have the idea that they must possess some necessary righteousness and goodness in order to gain God's favor. But that is law, not grace. How can you tell a shivering person to warm up *before* he comes to the fire? You will instead say to him to come to the fire and get warmed up. The Biblical order for us is not to stop sinning and then to believe, but to believe and then to refrain from sinning. Mephibosheth was formerly full of fear, but after he was graciously treated by David, he realized who he truly was. He said to the king, "What is thy servant, that thou shouldest look upon such a dead dog as I am?" (v.8)

I am reminded here of that statement in Romans which says, "not knowing that the goodness of God leadeth thee to repentance" (Rom. 2.4). Upon knowing the goodness and love of God, one will just naturally repent. When Mephibosheth came to the king, he hoped he could still return to the land of no pasture. But after he had tasted grace, he prostrated himself on the ground and repented. It was Mephibosheth who had erred, therefore he needed to repent. David had not erred, so he had no need to repent. God does not need to repent, but we do. Before Mephibosheth knew David loved him, David loved him; after he knew David loved him, David still loved him. So is God towards us. However, after we know the love of God, our mind and concept will undergo a change. Come to God just as you are because He has already loved you.

The Feet under the Table

Perhaps some may raise this question: Salvation is indeed based on grace and not on works, for God treats me just as David treated Mephibosheth; yet after being saved, should I not do good? Why is it that I feel sometimes up and sometimes down, sometimes good and sometimes bad? Before answering this question, please read this verse: "So Mephibosheth dwelt in Jerusalem; for he did eat continually at the king's table. And he was lame in both his feet" (v.13). The beginning of our salvation is grace, but so is the keeping of our salvation to be grace also. The error many commit is in thinking that grace begins our salvation but works maintain it thereafter. There is no such thing. We should recognize that whatever is the condition before salvation is the condition for preservation after salvation. I am saved through Jesus, and I am being kept to the end also by Jesus. Though Mephibosheth dined often with the king at his table, both his feet were still lame. If a person is only lame in *one* foot, he can still leap about, but if lame in *both* feet he cannot move at all. Let us see that the sitting at the king's table is real, but so is the lameness of both feet real too. The king will not have the lame man at his table merely for one day and then drive him away if he should still be lame after a few days.

Although your feet are lame, they are *under the table*. You can therefore eat whatever is on the table. So why as it were put your feet on the table? Just concentrate on what is on the table, for what God has provided there is good, rich, sweet, and nourishing. Eat to your heart's satisfaction. Do not look at *yourself*, but look at the riches which God has given you.

Every time we look at ourselves, we lose our peace. Human eyes are made to look outside, not to look inside. Introspection is not our portion. Our eyes should be fixed upon the Lord, and thus shall we be transformed from glory to glory according to His image. If we turn to look at ourselves, we will be like Mephibosheth seeing the lame feet. After we are saved, we receive a new life, and the Holy Spirit dwells in us. We are a new creation. Nevertheless, the self which comes from

Adam never changes. That is why, when the saintly Augustine was dying, he said this: "All the seeds of sin in the entire world are within me." As long as we are not freed from this body, our feet are yet lame. Let us not turn back to look at ourselves, but keep looking at the abundant grace which God has set on the table before us; and then shall our hearts be satisfied.

Mephibosheth towards David (16.1-4, 19.24-30)

Several years have now passed. In the meantime David's son Absalom had rebelled, and David had been forced to flee Jerusalem. When David was a little past the top of an ascent, Ziba, the servant of Mephibosheth, came forth with a couple of asses saddled, and upon them sat two hundred loaves of bread, a hundred clusters of raisins, a hundred of summer fruits, and a bottle of wine. "And the king said unto Ziba, What meanest thou by these? And Ziba said, The asses are for the king's household to ride on; and the bread and summer fruit for the young men to eat; and the wine, that such as are faint in the wilderness may drink. And the king said, And where is thy master's son? And Ziba said unto the king, Behold, he abideth at Jerusalem; for he said, Today will the house of Israel restore me the kingdom of my father. Then said the king to Ziba, Behold, thine is all that pertaineth unto Mephibosheth" (16.2-4a). Was all this true? By reading chapter 19 we shall know the truth of the matter.

After the rebellion of Absalom had been quelled, David returned to Jerusalem; and Mephibosheth, the grandson of Saul, came down to meet the king. From the day the king had departed until the day he had come home in peace, Mephibosheth had restrained himself from doing three things: he had "neither dressed his feet, nor trimmed his beard, nor washed his clothes" (v.24). Can we perceive what this means? This which we have just read is nothing less than the unveiling of the heart of a widow in Mephibosheth! For in essence he is saying that the David who treats me well is no longer here. And although no one comes to harm me, I have already lost interest in the world. What is the sense of beautifying myself? The king is not here; who, then, has the heart for any embellishment? The same sentiments would be echoed in the hearts of some rare believers today. They would say: We know how unworthy we are to be saved. This world has rejected our Savior and has crucified Him, and therefore we now live here with a widow's heart. The reason we can deny the world is not because of the unlovingness of the world but because our Lover is no longer here. Since all He himself got from the world was a tomb, how can we, His beloved ones, love the world? We feel the world is against us.

The heart of Mephibosheth was a widow's heart. The king was not there, so he lost interest in all things. A believer deep in the Lord once said, "Where Jesus is, there is heaven. If Jesus is in hell, hell is heaven; if Jesus is not in heaven, heaven is no longer heaven." When I first heard this, I thought, how could this be! But now, I can readily say this is indeed true. For previously we only thought of the problem of sin, but now we ponder the Lord Jesus. Formerly we thought of how to escape the penalty of hell, yet now we think of the Lord himself. Hence heaven is lovely because the Lord is there; but if the Lord were in hell, hell would become lovely too!

This world is but a wilderness. What is a wilderness? It is someplace desolate. This is not to say that the arts and natural sciences of this world are ugly; but because He is not here, these things amount to nothing. How can I love a world that despises the Lord Jesus? I have said before that wherever your lover is there is the happy place. Hence, clothes, food and drink may remain the same, yet these are not the same to you if your lover is absent. My home is Foochow, and I often think of going there. But what I desire is not Foochow itself, but the brothers and sisters of kindred spirit who are there. Together we have passed through affliction, poverty and persecution. If these brethren were not there, I would easily forget Foochow. And thus are we to be towards the world. Today the Lord is not here, therefore we cannot find rest or joy in this world. Our attitude towards the world should be that of a widow.

When Mephibosheth came down to meet the king, he was asked by David why he did not go with the king. His answer was:

> My lord, O king, my servant deceived me: for thy servant said, I will saddle me an ass, that I may ride thereon, and go with the king; because thy servant is lame. And he hath slandered thy servant unto my lord the king; but my lord the king is as an angel of God: do therefore what is good in thine eyes. For all my father's house were but dead men before my lord the king; yet didst thou set thy servant among them that did eat at thine own table. What right

therefore have I yet that I should cry any more unto the king? (vv.26-28)

In these words we find that Mephibosheth did not mention anything about bread and wine; he merely related
the fact of being deceived. His heart was satisfied with
the safe return of the king; what did it matter if he had
earlier been abused?

We realize that when a person tries to disclose his
heart, it actually does not depend on the words. For
a love slave of the Lord, his heart is more than his words
can express. The deeper the love, the more mysterious
it becomes. If you truly love the Lord, you may preserve
your purity in the midst of universal opposition. On
that day when we shall see the Lord face to face, we
will not tell Him how much we have forsaken for His
sake because we will not talk about ourselves. Rather,
we will say how regretful we are for not having loved
Him more and served Him more faithfully while on
earth. At that time, we shall truly feel that offering ten
thousand worlds to Him would still be too small a gift
for Him.

Apart from mentioning his having been deceived
by his servant Ziba, Mephibosheth said nothing else.
For his heart was occupied with one thing only, which
was that his king David had come back. Nothing else
mattered anymore. He is satisfied with simply sitting
at David's table. He does not need to explain nor ask
for revenge. As long as the king was back, Mephibosheth was satisfied.

"And the king said unto him, Why speakest thou
any more of thy matters? I say, Thou and Ziba divide

the land. And Mephibosheth said unto the king, Yea, let him take all, forasmuch as my lord the king is come in peace unto his own house" (vv.29,30). Each time I read this word of Mephibosheth, I say, Amen! What does it matter about my loss if the king has come back in peace? As long as my Lord is gaining, my loss is nothing to me. The whole question for Mephibosheth was whether he was peaceful, not whether that which David had given him was still there!

"Though he slay me, yet will I trust in him" (Job 13.15 AV). On the eve before he was strangled to death, a Christian martyr declared: "God, if You do not intervene, tomorrow I still will go blindfolded. Come heaven! Come hell!" Here was a hero of faith. His attitude was, "O Lord, You will never mistreat me. Yet even if it is Your pleasure to ill-treat me, I shall still take delight in Your ill-treatment. So long as You are pleased, even my suffering is most sweet."

David's own settlement of the matter was doubtless wrong, but our Lord will never wrong us. Nonetheless, in being wrongly treated, Mephibosheth's true heart was manifested: "Yea, let him take all, forasmuch as my lord the king is come in peace unto his own house." Here we see that God will save us to the point where we seek only His gain and not our own. God's gain or loss is real gain or loss; mine is nothing at all.

On one occasion I knew I should obey God, yet I just could not obey. Finally I told Him, "Please do not yield, wait until I yield." We ought to be the one who yields, not God. He who has once captured my heart has it forever. My heart is captured, and therefore my all is His. What is our expectation and pursuit before

God? Is it something for ourselves? or all for Him? May we hereafter reckon our all to be His. May we seek only His gain as our satisfaction.

David Preserved Mephibosheth (21.7)

"But the king spared Mephibosheth, the son of Jonathan the son of Saul, because of Jehovah's oath that was between them, between David and Jonathan, the son of Saul." This verse speaks of the end of this lame child. We need to recall that there was a famine in the days of David for three years. This famine was due to Saul and his bloody house on the occasion when he had put to death the Gibeonites. As atonement for this sin, the Gibeonites had asked that seven sons of Saul be delivered up to them to be hanged. The first one to be delivered would naturally have been Mephibosheth. But David spared him and delivered seven other sons of Saul. Therefore Mephibosheth was never killed. This can serve to illustrate how a saved person shall never perish. David never *purposely* treated Mephibosheth wrongly, so will God ever treat us wrongly? If David protected Mephibosheth from the beginning to the end, will not God keep us to the end?

"I give unto them eternal life; and they shall never perish, and no one shall snatch them out of my hand. My Father, who hath given them unto me, is greater than all; and no one is able to snatch them out of the Father's hand" (John 10.28,29). These are two familiar verses. They tell us so plainly that the reason none can snatch us away is because of "my hand . . . the Father's hand." The hand of the Lord Jesus and the hand of the heavenly Father hold us fast; who, then, can possibly snatch us from Their hands? There is absolutely none. Some may think it is true that none can snatch us but that we may escape ourselves. Whoever thinks that way betrays his ignorance of the gospel. Will not a father who holds the hand of his child tighten his grip when he sees a danger or when he notices the child himself is struggling to get away?

Once a black woman in America was saved and joyfully sang aloud, Once saved, forever saved! A half-believing Christian asked her whether in so singing she could be sure of going to heaven. So she recited the words of John 10.28,29 to him. He insinuated that although these words were true, she should not be too careless because the bigger the hand the greater the hole through which she might slip away. Her reply was, "I will never slip away because I am God's little finger." She really knew the Bible, for what she said is true, since the Lord is the head and we are the members of His body. We are joined to Him in Life. If a Christian can perish, then the body of Christ will forever be short and never full. May all Christians shout hallelujah to the Lord! Once saved, forever saved; therefore, give all to God.

5 | Saved Through Baptism

It came to pass, when men began to multiply on the face of the ground, and daughters were born unto them, that the sons of God saw the daughters of men that they were fair; and they took them wives of all that they chose. And Jehovah said, My Spirit shall not strive with man for ever, for that he also is flesh: yet shall his days be a hundred and twenty years. The Nephilim were in the earth in those days, and also after that, when the sons of God came in unto the daughters of men, and they bare children to them: the same were the mighty men that were of old, the men of renown. And Jehovah saw that the wickedness of man was great in the earth, and that every imagination of the thoughts of his heart was only evil continually. And it repented Jehovah that he had made man on the earth, and it grieved him at his heart. And Jehovah said, I will destroy man whom I have created from the face of the ground; both man and beast, and creeping things, and birds of the heavens; for it repenteth me that I have made them. But Noah found favor in the eyes of Jehovah. These are the generations of Noah. Noah was a righteous man, and perfect in his generations: Noah walked with God. (Gen. 6.1-9)

God remembered Noah, and all the beasts, and all the cattle that were with him in the ark. (Gen. 8.1a)

The ark rested in the seventh month, on the seventeenth day of the month, upon the mountains of Ararat. And the waters decreased continually until the tenth month: in the tenth month, on the first day of the month, were the tops of the mountains seen. (Gen. 8.4,5)

It came to pass in the six hundred and first year, in the first month, the first day of the month, the waters were dried up from off the earth: and Noah removed the covering of the ark, and looked, and, behold, the face of the ground was dried. And in the second month, on the seven and twentieth day of the month, was the earth dry. And God spake unto Noah, saying, Go forth from the ark, thou, and thy wife, and thy sons, and thy sons' wives with thee. Bring forth with thee every living thing that is with thee of all flesh, both birds, and cattle, and every creeping thing that creepeth upon the earth; that they may breed abundantly in the earth, and be fruitful, and multiply upon the earth. And Noah went forth, and his sons, and his wife, and his sons' wives with him. (Gen. 8.13-18)

Noah builded an altar unto Jehovah, and took of every clean beast and of every clean bird, and offered burntofferings on the altar. And Jehovah smelled the sweet savor; and Jehovah said in his heart, I will not again curse the ground any more for man's sake, for that the imagination of man's heart is evil from his youth; neither will I again smite any more everything living, as I have done. (Gen. 8.20,21)

> That aforetime were disobedient, when the longsuf-
> fering of God waited in the days of Noah, while the ark
> was a preparing, wherein few, that is, eight souls, were
> saved through water: which also after a true likeness doth
> now save you, even baptism, not the putting away of the
> filth of the flesh, but the interrogation of a good con-
> science toward God, through the resurrection of Jesus
> Christ. (1 Peter 3.20,21)
>
> He that believeth and is baptized shall be saved. (Mark
> 16.16a)

The story of Noah's ark is familiar to all. What we
would like to do is to learn what the Bible really shows
us in that story. In the matter of our salvation, the Bible
approaches it from several different angles: some of it
speaks of our position before God; some of it, of our
acceptance by God; some, of our communion with
God; and some, of our position with the world. All this
may sound complicated, so let us use some illustrations
to explain them.

Several Expressions of Salvation

The coats of skins mentioned in Genesis
3—"Jehovah God made for Adam and for his wife coats
of skins, and clothed them" (v.21)—expresses salvation.
But what aspect of salvation does it represent? It pic-
tures for us how we human beings may be justified
before God.

The offering of Abel told of in Genesis 4 also expresses an aspect of salvation. Now the offering of Cain
was rejected by God, but Abel's offering was accepted.

This is because Cain offered what was of himself, whereas Abel offered what was of God—even the lamb of atonement. All the proper sacrifices mentioned in the Scriptures are a reflection of God's acceptance of us human beings. The story, for example, of the prodigal son recorded in Luke 15 speaks of God's acceptance of sinners. The first chapter of Ephesians discloses how God accepts us in the beloved Son (1.6 AV). Likewise, too, the fourth chapter of Genesis with its narrative of Cain and Abel suggests this aspect of salvation, which is, God's acceptance of man. Even the rapture of Enoch spoken of in Genesis 5 reveals God's salvation—in this case, that aspect of it which denotes victory over death.

Thus Genesis 3 expresses that facet of God's salvation which the Bible elsewhere calls justification; Genesis 4 speaks of God's acceptance; and Genesis 5 stresses the matter of overcoming death. The ark in Genesis 6 also expresses salvation, only it deals with an aspect different from those of Genesis 3, 4 and 5. For it reflects the relationship of Christians to the world. How is a Christian to be delivered from all which is condemned by God? How is he to be released from all which is subject to God's judgment? We shall see how, through accepting God's salvation, we are freed from the condemnation and judgment of God.

Sin has its various aspects. That sin depicted for us in chapter 3 of Genesis is a sin against God—both a sin before Him and a sin that is rebellious against Him. Wherefore, in the very same chapter, we are told how such sin before God needs to be covered by the coats of skins provided by God, so that man can be justified before Him. The sin told of in chapter 4 is likewise a sin against God, but it is also one against man's neighbor. Cain committed the sin of murdering his brother. He violated the two greatest commandments of God: "Thou shalt love the Lord thy God with all thy heart, and with all thy soul, and with all thy mind"; and, "thou shalt love thy neighbor as thyself." Such sin requires sacrifice to be offered by man to God so as for him to be accepted. Even sin against man needs acceptance before God, otherwise that sin shall remain. The sin of Genesis chapter 5 is again different from the aforementioned sin since it tells of the sin of forgetting God. For by this time people had largely disregarded God and walked according to their own will. They ate their own meals and passed their days as they desired. Only one person at that time — Enoch — walked with God. The whole world was full of death because people did not want God. However, God redeemed Enoch completely from this deadly world so that he should not see death. Yet while the sin of chapter 5 was the sin of the multitudes, the sin delineated in chapter 6 was a corporate sin. It was a sin which was committed against God by the world of mankind as a "kosmos" — as one grand organized entity. Hence the world was its scope, and thus Genesis 6 tells of how the entire world system had sinned against God.

The Judgment of the Flood

At the inception of chapter 6 we discover that the fallen angels sinned together with fallen men. The "sons of God" spoken of here were the fallen angels and the "daughters of men" spoken of were the fallen men. Both had been created by God and both had spirit. But when they joined themselves together to sin, the world was bound to come to an end. Those who sinned in the first world were angels in the heavenlies; those who sinned in the second world were men on the earth. And when they sinned together, the end unquestionably was soon coming to pass. Sinful angels and sinful men would shortly be judged by God. Now man had become especially "flesh"—whether in doing good or in committing sin, it nonetheless was flesh. Therefore, God would not strive with man forever. Formerly the Spirit of God strove with man, but still man refused to hear the voice of God. Consequently, He finally gave man up. In other words, man had become so corrupted that the Spirit of God could not strive with him anymore, which meant that even the Holy Spirit could not change him. As a result, the Holy Spirit drew back and let the world go through judgment.

Please understand that your own flesh today is not any better than the flesh was in Noah's time. Unless we allow the flesh with its lusts and passions to be crucified, then the Holy Spirit has no way to work in us either. As in Noah's day, the Holy Spirit will not attempt to persuade man to reform, for he is beyond repair; He today can only try to convince man to be born again. The flesh can do nothing except to sin; the regenerated of God alone can do any good. Regeneration is not tears, confession or zeal; it is not being a good church member, reading the Bible, and praying; regeneration is the act of receiving a new life from above, that is, from God himself. In short, regeneration is a second birth.

If the world becomes full of sin, something must be done first before the Holy Spirit can commence to work. That first thing is for God to send the Lord Jesus to this world. Once man becomes a sinner, the Lord Jesus and not the Spirit must come first. Should the Holy Spirit come first, He can do nothing. Only after the Lord Jesus has the sinner judged will the Holy Spirit be able to work. Hence, the first of the many parables found in Luke chapter 15 is that of the shepherd — the Lord Jesus — seeking the lost sheep. The second parable is the woman — the Holy Spirit — who sweeps the house to find the lost piece of silver. Without the redemptive work of Christ, the Holy Spirit can do nothing. If the work of Christ remains unfinished, the work of the Holy Spirit cannot commence. But since the work of Christ is already done, the Holy Spirit is now able to work. Accordingly, in Genesis 6 we have delineated for us first the work of redemption, and only then in Genesis 8 do we observe the dove which expresses the work of the Holy Spirit.

"The end of all flesh is come before me; for the earth is filled with violence through them; and, behold, I will destroy them with the earth" (Gen. 6.13). God saw that the earth was filled with violence and sins, that it was corrupted to the core. So, He declared that its end had come. There was no other way but to bring all before Him to an end. God judged them all and destroyed all flesh — both of men and of living things — by the universal flood.

What many Christians fail to realize is the position of the world before God. Today when the brothers and sisters are exhorted to be separated from the world, it is almost as though it were as difficult as trying to snatch away a piece of chocolate from a child's mouth. It appears so hard because of the fact that Christians do not discern the position the world has before God. Let us recognize that salvation has not only its personal aspect but also its corporate aspect, just as sin too has its corporate dimension as well as its personal dimension. The people who crucified the Lord Jesus at Calvary were not only the Jews but the whole world as well. Those at enmity with God at that time were not merely Jews, they included all and everything that constituted the entire world system.

Let us take, for example, the enmity between two nations: is it something personal or corporate? We of course know that this cannot be termed a personal relationship. If some person in one of the two countries was to treat somebody in the opposite country well, then this would be a personal relationship. But today it is not a matter of being good or bad on the part of one or several individuals in one country towards one or several individuals in the other, such as in the case of a personal animosity emerging as a result of one person's parents being killed by one or several people from the enemy country; it is instead a matter of the whole country standing as an enemy nation. It is a corporate antagonism between country and country. So that here is not a speaking of one individual but a speaking of the entire world system — including its organization, customs and reputations — as the enemy of God. As long as you and I are part of that world system, we are an enemy of God, from which we need to be delivered. And once having seen this, you and I will not be found exhorting people to reform or change, for we know that all these are useless. In the eyes of God, the entire world system—the "kosmos" itself—is corrupted. So that God is at enmity with the world, and the world is at enmity with Him. All who love the world do not love God, and the love of God cannot be in their hearts. All who befriend the world just naturally become enemies of God. And this is precisely the way God perceives it.

Let me ask you, do you want to be delivered from hell, which is the lake of fire? I believe we all desire to be delivered from such a destiny and to enter New Jerusalem. Many expect to be saved and to go to heaven. And this aspect of salvation is called, in the Bible, justification and acceptance by God. Yet there is another aspect of salvation which Biblically can be termed deliverance from the world. Deliverance from the world actually goes hand in hand with deliverance from the lake of fire.

The Bible tells us God found but one man, Noah. The first man Adam had been corrupted and had come to his end. Nothing could be done with him. So God found another man, and this second man was Noah. Noah was accepted by God, and he served as a type of Christ. Through him, God set up a way of salvation by which to save people from the world. God ordered him to build an ark with gopher wood and bring all kinds of living creatures, birds, cattle, creeping things—each after its kind—to the ark. He then caused rain to fall upon the earth till the whole earth was deluged. Who were the saved? Those who were delivered from the world by staying in the ark. Those who were delivered from the world were those delivered from the flood. In like manner, therefore, whoever is delivered from the world is delivered from the lake of fire. For it is not sinners who are going to hell but the people of the world who are. Preachers often say sinners go to hell, but actually they should say that the world goes to hell. As long as you are among those of the world, you are destined to go to hell.

Once I met a man on a boat. He asked me: "What kind of person is qualified for hell?" My reply to him was: "People such as you should go to hell." I said this to him because all mankind must go to hell. To be saved means you are saved from the perishing federation. Although we are not all criminals we nonetheless are all sinners, for the Bible says that all men are sinners. You and I may not commit a certain sin or violate some special law, and therefore we are not criminals; yet all of us are sinners. To be saved from the world is to be saved from the world which is under God's judgment.

The Salvation of the Ark

At the time of the Deluge, Noah and living creatures —birds, cattle and creeping things—were saved. Noah as well as the ark typify the Savior. But whereas Noah is a type of the Son of God, the ark stands as a type of the Son of Man because it is made of gopher wood, it thus representing the human nature of the Lord Jesus. Those who were saved in the Deluge were manifested to be those who were saved from the world. As all the fountains of the great deep were broken up and the windows of heaven were opened, the whole world, and not just some individuals, was condemned. Consequently, to be saved is to be saved from the world federation. All who are in the Ark of God are saved, that is to say, they are saved out of the world. Today a saved person cannot be saved and yet remain in the world, even as no one in Noah's day could have had one foot in the ark and one foot in the world: all who entered Noah's ark were shut into the ark.

Since that day, therefore, it is impossible for a saved person to love the world on the one hand and to love the Lord on the other. Although you may do so stealthily, you are not permitted so to do by God. One who believes in the Lord must wholly reject the world and not love it. Do not fancy you can change things to make them less worldly, because salvation means God has fundamentally already taken you *out* of the world. And since you are outside the world, you ought, accordingly, to live such a life. Now this which has just been said is something quite different from exhorting people not to love the world. Countrymen of one nation hate the people of an enemy country not because their faces were slapped by their adversaries but because hostility exists between the two countries. And such is now our problem.

As we have said, we are a people who have been delivered from the world. Yet how are we delivered? God shows us that since the world is occupied by the enemy and it thus opposes Him, He saves us out of it. He as it were "builds" an ark in the person of his Son and brings people out of the world into His Ark. In Noah's day God caused all the living things upon the earth to die except for what He kept both of men and living things in the ark through the death of the flood, and then He released them to fill the new world. So that what is illustrated here is that the old federal head Adam and all who were in Adam were rejected by God, and only the new federal head Noah and all who were in Noah would manifest new life with their seeds replenishing the entire earth.

Now those who were in the new earth of Noah's day typify all who in the future day shall inherit the new heaven and the new earth because they are in Christ. The people who were in the ark represent the people of our day who are in Christ. Accordingly, all who are in Christ are those who shall be in the future new heaven and new earth. Those who were outside the ark of Noah represent those people who are in Adam, and therefore they are the people who will be judged by God in the future. On the other hand, those who had entered the ark were brought through the judgment of water and entered and filled the new earth. And this can explain how Christ is to fill the future new heaven and new earth.

"The ark rested . . . upon the mountains of Ararat." Ararat means "holy land." It thus stands for resurrection — the coming out of death. It also speaks of the ascension of our Lord Jesus. As the ark rested upon the mountains of Ararat, their tops were seen. It only awaited the moment for the ground to become dry. Likewise, we are today resting on the mountains of Ararat, having seen their peaks and waiting for the ground to dry. Because our Lord has died, been resurrected, and has ascended, we wait until God has finished His judgment upon the earth.

The Ark and Baptism

What we would like to focus on, however, is not this that we have briefly touched upon above, but rather to lay stress on the matter of baptism. We have seen what Noah did and how he and his family passed through death by entering and remaining in the ark until they inherited the new earth. In 1 Peter 3 we learn that the ark, in passing through water, expresses the act of New Testament baptism. The waters of the Deluge signify the water of baptism: "[who] that aforetime were disobedient, when the longsuffering of God waited in the days of Noah, while the ark was a preparing, wherein few, that is, eight souls, were saved through water: which also after a true likeness doth now save you, even baptism, not the putting away of the filth of the flesh, but the interrogation of a good conscience toward God, through the resurrection of Jesus Christ" (vv.20,21). How are we saved and what saves us? Baptism saves us. Are you surprised at my saying this? Does baptism indeed save people? May I frankly tell you that unless we are baptized we cannot be saved. For Peter likewise declared that the baptism as typified by the flood saves us through the resurrection of Jesus Christ. Mark 16.16a declares that "he that believeth and is baptized shall be saved."

How we change Mark 16.16a to read: "He that believeth and is saved shall be baptized." The Bible, though, puts baptism before salvation. And thus we become confused. Our view is that only the saved can be baptized. Yet the word of God asserts that without baptism there is no salvation—that "he that . . . is baptized shall be saved." In short, a person is saved because he has been baptized.

Please do not misunderstand the meaning of being saved through baptism. For the Bible tells us of *various* aspects of salvation, not just one. Justification, for example, is that aspect which emphasizes man's position before God; the aspect of God's acceptance of man emphasizes the difference between the believing ones and the sinners; forgiveness, the remission of our past transgressions; and eternal life, the disparity between us and death. But the aspect of salvation as represented by baptism emphasizes *our relationship with the world.* For salvation speaks not merely of our escaping hell in the future; according to its *strictest* interpretation, salvation points to our deliverance from the world today.

Who will know you are saved? Who will know you as being of Christ? You may readily say you are saved, yet you are not able to open yourself up and expose your faith to people. We as human beings are unable to see man's inward faith. Only God can see faith in man. He knows you are already justified, accepted by Him, that your sins have been forgiven and you have received eternal life. But men do not know all this. James asserts that men cannot see faith; they can only see works. Hence the first work every Christian must do before men is to undergo baptism.

The first act before *God* is to "believe," but the first act before *men* is to be "baptized." To be baptized is to come out of the world and enter into Christ. It is to come out of the house and enter the ark. Baptism is a declaring—as Noah did in his day—that the judgment, wrath and punishment of God have fallen on the world because it resists and rejects Him. Baptism is also a declaring that we are not willing to be ranked among the people of the world but will come out of them and enter the Ark that God has prepared for us. Accordingly, baptism is not a ritual of having water sprinkled upon us or of our being immersed. It is rather a declaration that there is no longer any relationship between the world and us since you and I have been delivered from the world.

The real meaning of baptism lies in the fact that we who formerly lived in the world are now dead and shall never rise again because of the judgment which Jesus Christ has suffered for us. Though physically we are in the water for but one or two minutes, spiritually speaking, it means *we* shall never come up out of the water again. From the viewpoint of the world, we are hereafter separated forever from it. We have no part with it. Our parents, wives and children are dearest to us. Yet if they are dead, they will be put away. They will not be taken out of their graves and kept in their house with the living. Similarly, in the eyes of the world, Christians are looked upon as being dead and buried.

The world is composed of two sizeable federations: one is the men of the world, the other is the saved ones in Christ. To be saved is to come out of the world federation which opposes God, is sinful and unclean, and to enter into the Christ federation. And therefore, we must be baptized, because baptism can save. (Of course, one must first *believe* in the Lord; otherwise he cannot be saved). According to Mark 16.16, to be baptized is to be liberated. Baptism thus stands as a great liberating force from this world and all that is of it. Yet baptism is even more than a liberation, it is also an entry; through baptism we enter into Christ because it is a being baptized into His death.

The Bible declares that all who believe have eternal life. This fact of spiritual life is due to the blood of the Lord Jesus; and this is irrefutable. But to be saved from the world is due to our entering into the Ark of God. And baptism serves as a demonstration of the fact that we have indeed come out of the world federation. Should someone ask you, for example, if you have really believed in the Lord, you should say, "I truly do believe in the Lord Jesus, and through His blood my sins are forgiven." For the Scriptures declare that "he that hath the Son hath the life" (1 John 5.12). You are very clear about this. But suppose you lose your temper and fight with some brothers. You may ask yourself after this incident whether you still believe and are saved. Your answer comes forth in the strongest affirmative, you not having the slightest doubt about it. Nevertheless, these brothers will doubt about your salvation. How is it? Let me now observe that many people are most certainly qualified to live in *heaven* but they are not qualified to live on *earth*. They are able to live before God but not competent to live at home. Allow me to say, therefore, that you should not permit people to baptize you merely on the ground of your saying you believe. You ought to know what baptism truly expresses before you are ever baptized. You ought to know you have been delivered from the world, because baptism is that action which declares to the entire world that you are no longer joined to it and are no longer standing with it because you have been emancipated from it. Baptism declares that henceforth you and I stand on the side of Christ.

I am not pressing you today to be baptized; I simply want you to understand before you receive baptism that the world federation and the Christ federation stand as opposing camps and that there is no ground of negotiation between them. Ages ago at the time of Noah, God had declared that the world was His enemy, that it was at enmity with Him. In the face of this reality, the salvation He provided was the ark; and all who entered it thereafter stood on God's side, they having capitulated to Him. And hence the Bible quite amazingly explains to us that the entering of the ark in order to pass through the flood now signifies and expresses baptism.

I would consequently speak not merely to those who are yet to be baptized but to all brothers and sisters in Christ: Today many of you have already been baptized. Yet why *were* you baptized? Was it because baptism to you is only a church procedure? Merely a church ritual? Or perhaps a command of the Bible? Or even that it is an appropriate expression of a Christian? Or a matter of following what other Christians have done? In contrast to all these explanations, let us ever keep in mind that basically baptism is a turning our backs towards the world and a turning of our faces towards Christ. It is a leaving of the world federation and a joining with the Christ federation. And between these two — between the world and Christ — there is no middle ground. For let us not forget that there was a door in Noah's ark. And that spiritually speaking, within the door is Christ but without the door is the world. If you would see this at your baptism, you would have no need for people to tell you how you must change a little here and change a little there. For your leaving the world is not as though it were a pulling out of a hair or two from your head, but a shaving off of *all* the hairs. Unfortunately, though, many believers have not seen this.

We are often thinking of how we may change this world; but God's intent is to judge this world and give us a new one. No human ways such as religious doctrine, literature, science, philosophy or ethical teaching can change this world. God has shown us that in spite of the loveliness and enjoyment this world gives, it nonetheless is His enemy. So that if you are still loving this world and living according to the world, it is because you have hope that the world will change. Yet God has no other way to deal with the world than to judge it.

The world of Noah's day became new through the washing judgment of the universal flood. In that day, God washed the world with water; and in the future day He will burn it with fire. Are we today like Lot who lingered in Sodom and Gomorrah which were ready to be burned? Or are we those who are unmoved by the world's blandishments. How sad that many are like Lot's wife living in and according to the world. Like her, are we the willing inhabitants of the earth, or are we those who let everything of this world pass us by because our expectation is the new heaven and the new earth where righteousness dwells?

"A light [a window] shalt thou make to the ark" (Gen. 6.16a). This Hebrew word here translated as "light" is used 24 times throughout the Old Testament, of which on 23 occasions it is translated as "noon" (that is to say, twelve noon)—although here it is translated as "light" or "window." So that the light spoken of here does not signify a small amount of light but a fullness of light, which is to say that it bespeaks a living in the Light of God.

"He That Believeth and Is Baptized Shall Be Saved"

At this point I would say a few words to the un-saved. You need to realize that we humans cannot change the world. God will instead judge this world; such is quite certain. How, then, can you prepare to escape God's judgment? Please note that the ark was pitched within and without with pitch. This word "pitch" in the original is the same Hebrew word translated as "atonement." Hence the word "pitch" betokens the atoning of sin; in other words, it signifies the covering of sin. The pitching of the ark within and without with pitch speaks of the atonement made by the Lord Jesus. Having the ark pitched within and without means that through the atonement by the blood of Christ the lives inside the Ark of God—Christ himself—are preserved. Outside Noah's ark—that is, in the world—was the flood, and all in the world died of that flood. Inside it, however, the ark was dry and clean. Spiritually speaking, today all our punishments have fallen on God's Ark—Christ—while none has fallen on us. Whoever looks for peace, forgiveness and salvation has but one way to go: to walk into the divine Ark.

Although the world is full of the judgment of God, you who are believers should know that Noah's ark had been pitched within and without with pitch, which today represents the redemptive work of Christ. And if you are in the Ark of God, not a drop of God's judgment on the world will fall on you. Suppose someone in the ark of old — say, the wife of Japheth or Noah's wife — had wept and cried aloud, "What if the ark should leak or sink?" We would today laugh at her! Yet let me ask you, If you consider the redemptive work of Christ to be real, if you believe the Lord Jesus was crucified to redeem you, why, then, do you not dare to say you are saved? —why are you still uneasy? For perhaps you too speculate, What if the blood of the Lord Jesus should lose its effectiveness? What if the divine Ark should leak? If this is your thinking, then I need to ask you if you really *do* trust in the finished work of Christ.

Once a person came to Dwight L. Moody with tears in his eyes. When asked the reason, he answered, "I am afraid of perishing. I have believed in the Lord but what must I do in order not to perish?" Mr. Moody responded by observing that the Bible makes clear that "he that believeth hath eternal life" (John 6.47), that "him that cometh to me I will in no wise cast out" (John 6.37), that "he is able to save to the uttermost them that draw near unto God through him" (Heb.7.25). Moody used Scripture verses like these while he talked with the man, but after two or three hours this man's problem was still unresolved. He insisted he truly believed in the Lord but that he was afraid of perdition. To which Moody replied: "Now I am beginning to think you are like one of Noah's daughters-in-law who might have cried in the ark out of fear lest it leaked." Upon hearing this, the man retorted by saying: "Mister, there is no such thing, for the ark is unleakable!" "But you are that very person," said Moody, "who cries in the ark of safety because you are afraid it may leak." Now as the man heard this, he immediately understood the implication and realized how faithless he had been.

The Lord Jesus is able to save to the very end all who approach God through Him. There is no difference between the wise and the foolish. To be saved or to remain unsaved depends on whether or not one is in God's ark. It has nothing to do with whether a person is most wise or most foolish, whether one is wealthy or quite poor. Those are not relevant issues at all because the one and only question is, are you or are you not in God's Ark of Refuge? Those who depend on the work of Christ and enter the divine Ark are saved. As many lives as there are today in the ark— that is, in Christ—exactly that many will be those who are kept by God in the future.

If you want to be a real Christian, you must—like Noah and his family—be in God's ark and not on the ground. You cannot be saved by your works. But you must tell the Lord, "Whatever is of the world is not mine, for I stand on Your side." Alas, many have believed in the Lord, yet they have not severed themselves from whatever comes from the world. May you be faithful to what you have done at baptism.

Finally, let us be clear that the water of baptism does not save, it is the death and resurrection of the Lord Jesus which saves. Baptism is that which expresses our salvation. The blood of the Lord Jesus saves us before God, and the water of baptism saves us from the world.

6 | Food for God's People

They shall eat the flesh in that night, roast with fire, and unleavened bread; with bitter herbs they shall eat it. Eat not of it raw, nor boiled at all with water, but roast with fire; its head with its legs and with the inwards thereof. (Ex. 12.8,9)

The whole congregation of the children of Israel murmured against Moses and against Aaron in the wilderness: and the children of Israel said unto them, Would that we had died by the hand of Jehovah in the land of Egypt, when we sat by the flesh-pots, when we did eat bread to the full; for ye have brought us forth into this wilderness, to kill this whole assembly with hunger. Then said Jehovah unto Moses, Behold, I will rain bread from heaven for you; and the people shall go out and gather a day's portion every day, that I may prove them, whether they will walk in my law, or not. (Ex. 16.2-4)

When the dew that lay was gone up, behold, upon the face of the wilderness a small round thing, small as the hoarfrost on the ground. And when the children of Israel saw it, they saith one to another, What is it? for they knew not what it was. And Moses said unto them, It is the bread which Jehovah hath given you to eat. This is the thing which Jehovah hath commanded. Gather ye of it every man according to his eating; an omer a head, according to the number of your persons, shall ye take it, every man for them that are in his tent. (Ex. 16.14-16)

All the congregation of the children of Israel journeyed from the wilderness of Sin, by their journeys, according to the commandment of Jehovah, and encamped in Rephidim: and there was no water for the people to drink. Wherefore the people strove with Moses, and said, Give us water that we may drink. And Moses said unto them, Why strive ye with me? wherefore do ye tempt Jehovah? And the people thirsted there for water; and the people murmured against Moses, and said, Wherefore hast thou brought us out of Egypt, to kill us and our children and our cattle with thirst? And Moses cried unto Jehovah, saying, What shall I do unto this people? they are almost ready to stone me. And Jehovah said unto Moses, Pass on before the people, and take with thee of the elders of Israel; and thy rod, wherewith thou smotest the river, take in thy hand, and go. Behold, I will stand before thee there upon the rock in Horeb; and thou shalt smite the rock, and there shall come water out of it, that the people may drink. And Moses did so in the sight of the elders of Israel. And he called the name of the place Massah, and Meribah, because of the striving of the children of Israel, and because they tempted Jehovah, saying, Is Jehovah among us, or not? (Ex. 17.1-7)

We remember the fish, which we did eat in Egypt for nought; the cucumbers, and the melons, and the leeks, and the onions, and the garlic: but now our soul is dried away; there is nothing at all save this manna to look upon. (Num. 11.5,6)

Today we would like to touch upon the subject of the food that the people of God eat. In looking into the record of Exodus, we can see that there are three kinds of food for God's people: first, the flesh of the lamb which is mentioned in chapter 12; second, the manna which is mentioned in chapter 16; and third, the water which came out of the rock told about in chapter 17. These were the kinds of food and drink with which God provided the children of Israel. These were all necessary; none could be missing. It would not have been well had they had the flesh of the lamb but no manna and water; neither could they have lived with manna but no water. With the flesh of the lamb plus the manna and the water, they were brought out of Egypt, went through the wilderness, and entered Canaan.

The Flesh of the Lamb

Let us first consider the lamb. The Bible tells us explicitly that the lamb points to our Lord Jesus. The children of Israel not only put the blood of the lamb on the doorposts, they also ate its flesh. We not only have our sins borne by the Lamb of God and thus escape perdition but we also accept Him to be our inner strength. Hence we must accept Him as well as believe in Him.

We notice from the account given how the children

of Israel were delivered from the hand of the Destroyer by the placement of the blood of the lamb on the outside of the door and how they gained strength to march out of Egypt through eating the flesh of the lamb. Today some have indeed believed in the Lord, yet they do not have the strength to forsake the world as typified in the Bible by Egypt. This is because they have not taken the flesh of God's Lamb into them. True, the blood has already been put on the doorposts of their hearts, but they have no strength to exit from worldly Egypt. Accordingly, the strength to obey the Lord and to follow His way depends on our eating flesh, not on the blood.

Exodus 12.8 informs us that the flesh of the lamb had to have been eaten on that same night of the exit of God's people out of Egypt. Though the word of God plainly says this, the experience of many of God's people nevertheless seems to be different. You ask a person today if he has believed in the Lord and has had his sins forgiven, and he may clearly and quickly give you an affirmative answer. But if you were to ask again, Why, then, do you love the world so much?, he might reply, "I do not have the strength to deny the world." (Quite possibly for him the scope of the world which he admires and cannot forsake is very limited, it perhaps being only a few people or a few tens of dollars). Now the reason for his inadequacy is due to his failure to eat the flesh "that very night" and thus be delivered from the bondage of Egypt. The meaning of eating flesh is to accept the Lord Jesus to our hearts to be our Savior. This will give us deliverance in our practical daily living.

On the one hand, we may speak of other Christians

as to why their lives have undergone such a change and are so holy after they had believed in the Lord Jesus, and on the other hand we may ask why it is that the world still has so much attraction for us who have also believed. Let us clearly see that for a believer to be delivered from the world the basis lies not in putting on the blood, but in eating the flesh. All believers have put on the blood of God's Lamb; what differentiates them one from another is this eating of the flesh.

How should the flesh be eaten? Verse 8 tells us that two things were to be taken with the flesh of the lamb. First was *the bitter herbs*. "Bitter herb" is not a name of a particular herb; this phrase merely describes the taste of an herb. So that whatever herb was bitter was to be used. The word bitter signifies that which is displeasing to the heart. And hence the spiritual meaning here is for a person to repent of his past sins or faults. Second was *the unleavened bread*. According to the New Testament, in Paul's first letter to the Corinthians, the meaning of unleavened bread is the putting away of sins (see 5.7,8). Thus, on the one hand there is to be the repenting of past trespasses, and on the other hand there is to be the forsaking of present sinful deeds. No one can hold on to sin with the one hand and hold on to God with the other. All who in their hearts desire after Egypt are unable to exit from Egypt. Hence the forsaking of present faults must accompany the repenting of past mistakes. Without purging out the leaven, even the eating of the flesh of the lamb will not get one out of Egypt.

How often we feel bad after having spoken a wrong word. Yet Satan will suggest that we are wrong all the time. But we should say, I would rather stand on God's side and not be a companion of Satan; I will not mind my dignity but will confess to whoever I have spoken the wrong word that I have been wrong. Such a reaction is to treat the past with bitter herbs and to face the future with unleavened bread, thus qualifying ourselves to eat the flesh of the lamb. The reason the spiritual life of many believers makes no progress is because they are not willing to repent and to put away their past sins. Whoever refuses to get rid of their past sins but returns there instead can never advance in the spiritual course.

Manna

Is it enough, though, to eat the flesh of the lamb? No, it is not enough. Yes, you have come out of Egypt, but ahead of you you have the wilderness journey on which to travel. In the wilderness you need to eat daily. The eating of the flesh of the lamb occurs but once because it typifies your initial need of accepting the Lord Jesus as your Savior only once. For the journey ahead, however, you need *daily* food to give you *daily* strength. We must recognize the fact that we must have strength to meet the work, the events, the affairs, and the battles of each day. What, then, is the food? In the New Testament, John 6 tells us it is the Lord who is our Manna from heaven. Let me ask you: since you have accepted the Lord Jesus as your Savior, how many times have you experienced Him as your daily manna? This is most important. No one expecting to survive physically can eat one meal and then eat no more. He must eat *daily*. Yet the same is true in the matter of our spiritual survival. No one can eat the flesh of the lamb just once at passover, and then eat no more. He must eat the daily bread; otherwise, he will die in the wilderness of his spiritual journey, never making any progress.

What is this daily food? Is it reading the Bible? It may look like it, but it is not. Is it prayer? Again, it seems to be so, but still it is not. Is it waiting on the Lord? No, it is not that either. All these are but *means*, the reality is the power of Christ. Through these means we draw on that power. Why should we read the Bible in the morning? Is it merely to understand the Scriptures? If that is the only reason for our morning reading, how pitiful we must be. We rise up early to read the Bible in order to gain the power of Christ for the day's living. Why do we get up in the morning to spend half an hour or an hour in prayer? It is to draw nigh to God and absorb the power of His life for our inner strength.

Let me illustrate this with a real case. There was a sister who served the Lord. She was most afraid of water buffaloes and dogs; yet if anyone ever goes to the villages to preach the gospel, he cannot avoid these two creatures. Now it so happened that whenever this sister saw a fat, black water buffalo, she would immediately flee. Once, even, she was walking along a country road when all of a sudden a few dogs barked at her from behind and a herd of water buffalo came towards her at the front! She was frightened to death! In trying to avoid the dogs, she met the buffaloes; and in attempting to avoid the buffaloes, she had to face the dogs.

And besides this, the road was quite narrow. Being thus caught on the horns of a dilemma, she nearly fainted. But at that very moment she prayed, "Lord, You are my life, give me strength." With each step she prayed that prayer, and she passed the twelve terrible water buffaloes safely. Now that is what I would call absorbing the strength of the Lord!

I have a friend who prays an excellent prayer each morning. He humbly declares: "God, I offer myself once again to you this day." I asked him what he offered himself to God for. He promptly answered, "I offer myself to God for Him to fill me." This is indeed a most excellent prayer to pray each morning of our lives.

Without such contact as this in the morning, where can the strength come for the day? Hence reading the Bible is essential to gain Christ, prayer is also necessary to absorb divine power. Yet what exactly is this action of absorbing power? It can be likened to our taking of meals time and time again, thus assimilating in our bodies the food we ingest that becomes our physical strength. So too is it in relation to our spiritual strength; it must be renewed daily. Sometimes our prayer is most sweet; and this is spiritual manna to our hearts. By contacting God each day, we gain spiritual strength to travel one day's journey.

Now the Bible also informs us that the manna of old was not to be left overnight for the next day's use. The spiritual lesson to be drawn from this is that each day there must be a new meeting with God for new strength. We need to cultivate this *daily* habit of gathering manna — that is, we must receive from God a daily new message, a daily new influence, a daily new portion of Christ. This is a good daily habit to have. We need to cultivate now the habit of gathering manna and absorbing power. We recognize how futile it is if we only know the Bible but not Christ. Let us therefore seek after this precious experience of knowing Christ as our Manna from heaven.

At the beginning we quoted Numbers 11.5 and 6 in which the children of Israel murmured, saying: "We remember the fish, which we did eat in Egypt for nought; the cucumbers, and the melons, and the leeks, and the onions, and the garlic; but now our soul is dried away; there is nothing at all save this manna to look upon." One thing will always be certain: whenever we grow tired of manna, the food of Egypt will appear before us. The leeks and onions and garlics of Egypt are very strong in taste. In fact, all the food of Egypt had a potent flavor. Things with strong flavor can always easily be recalled. How strange that what the children of Israel remembered were these eatable things, whereas they easily forgot the many afflictions in Egypt—such as the male children having been thrown into the river, the making of bricks amidst harsh conditions, and the cruel beatings perpetrated by their overseers. Many who fall often forget the bitterness of sin, the bondage of Satan, and the struggle of the past; they only recall how they could do anything they wanted to do before they had believed in the Lord Jesus but that now they feel bound and miserable. In one sense their memory is quite good because they remember a lot, yet their memory is also poor in that they forget even their deliverance and salvation.

One reason why Christians cannot bear fruit is because they too easily forget how they were initially rescued and saved. The fact of the matter is that it really is not fatal to not have those smelly foods such as leeks and onions and garlic, but it is vital to have the manna. All who begin to grow weary of getting close to Christ have already thought of Egypt and of the potent flavor of onions and garlic. For this reason, each Christian must keep receiving his daily manna. It is simply not adequate to eat a little manna solely on the Lord's day or every three or five days as many Christians seem to be doing. But if we touch the Lord day by day, we shall find that such a touch is truly our strength.

The Water Out of the Rock

Eating the flesh of the lamb is the beginning of life, eating manna is the maintenance of life to grow, and drinking water is to enjoy life. The meaning of water lies in its power to awaken, to refresh, and to give renewed strength. The flesh of the lamb gives us life, that is to say, Christ lives in us. But the Christ who lives in us needs to be nourished by the Christ on the throne in order to have the strength for the rest of the pilgrimage. However, if there are only these two elements — flesh and manna — there can be no enjoyment, and the Christian's face will become long and he will pass the day sadly just as did the children of Israel in complaining that their soul had dried up because they had nothing to look upon save the manna. It is therefore essential to have water for enjoyment.

How did the water make its appearance in the lives

of God's people of old? According to Exodus 17.5, the
first action was for Moses to take up the old rod which
the passage describes as the one "wherewith [Moses]
smotest the river"; it was not to be taken up as "the
rod of God." God's description of the rod in these terms
was for the purpose of reminding the children of Israel
about the earlier act of Moses in Egypt of striking the
river. When the water of Egypt was smitten by the rod
of God, the water turned into blood. And blood meant
death. This for us today serves to indicate that all the
enjoyments and pleasures of Egypt were under the judgment of God. All the amusements of this present age,
in fact, are but blood. Perhaps in the eyes of the Egyptians many things were quite enjoyable, but to us these
things are but blood. For this reason, some complain
that being a Christian subjects a person to much bondage. Does the Christian have things to enjoy? Certainly,
yet their nature is different from that of the things which
the Egyptians enjoyed. And hence God had to bring
out the rod used back in Egypt.

We have already seen that life comes from Christ,
and even the maintenance of life is also of Christ. But
where comes joy? Some mothers take their children as
enjoyment. Our joy, though, comes from the smitten
rock. God said to Moses: "Behold, I will stand before
thee there upon the rock in Horeb [Horeb is one of the
peaks in the wilderness of Sinai]; and thou shalt smite
the rock, and there shall come water out of it, that the
people may drink" (17.6). So that the spiritual water
we have flows from the Rock that is before God. And
according to 1 Corinthians 10, this Rock is Christ
himself (v.4). The smiting of the rock speaks of the

death of Christ; and the water which flows out has reference to the Holy Spirit. Hence our joy and enjoyment are all to be found in the Holy Spirit. This joy more than compensates for any loss of ours. Oftentimes in the dark days of our lives our knees may tremble and our hands may hang down. There is nothing for us to enjoy. But at the very same time God will give us joy which fully compensates all our loss.

The prophet Isaiah once spoke of our Lord as One who grew up before God as "a root out of a dry ground" (53.2). What can this mean? A root cannot grow in dry ground; consequently, this metaphor was used to show us that what the Lord Jesus relied on when on this earth was God, for the world could not give Him any supply. And so shall we who follow Christ also be in this world. To drink of this world is to drink the blood of death; yet not to drink of this world is to remain thirsty; but Christ is the Living Water that can quench all our thirst and grant us full satisfaction.

Today God stands on the mount before the smitten Rock, and thus spiritual joy for us is not something vague but is directly before us. How great is our God! For indeed, many times before we end up weeping we have already begun to smile and to laugh.

7 | A Believer's Value Before God

Scripture Reading: Exodus 30.11-16, Leviticus 27.1-8

During the Old Testament period each time a person's life was to be numbered before God, he needed a sin-offering lest he be subject to a plague: "Jehovah spake unto Moses, saying, When thou takest the sum of the children of Israel, according to those that are numbered of them, then shall they give every man a ransom for his soul unto Jehovah, when thou numberest them; that there be no plague among them, when thou numberest them" (Ex. 30.11,12). It is for this reason that God was displeased with David and sent a plague upon the children of Israel when the king ordered Joab to number the Israelites (see 1 Chron. 21). Whoever is without the blood will be instantly judged.

Several points are raised in this passage from Exodus 30: (1) "Jehovah spake unto Moses, saying, When thou takest the sum of the children of Israel, according to those that are *numbered* of them, then shall they

give every man a *ransom* for his soul unto Jehovah,
when thou numberest them; that there be no plague
among them, when thou numberest them" (vv.11,12);
(2) "This they shall give, every one that passeth over
unto them that are numbered; *half a shekel* after the
shekel of the sanctuary . . . for an offering to Jehovah"
(v.13); (3) " . . . them that are numbered, *from twenty
years old and upward*, shall give the offering of
Jehovah" (v.14); and (4) "The rich shall *not give more*,
and the poor shall *not give less*, than the half shekel,
when they give the offering of Jehovah, to make atonement for your souls" (v.15).

Likewise several points are raised in the passage
from Leviticus 27: (1) "Jehovah spake unto Moses, saying, Speak unto the children of Israel, and say unto
them, When a man shall *accomplish a vow*, the persons shall be for Jehovah by *thy estimation*" (vv.1,2);
(2) "thy estimation shall be of the male from twenty
years old even unto sixty years old, even thy estimation shall be fifty shekels of silver, after the shekel of
the sanctuary. And if it be a female, then thy estimation shall be thirty shekels. And if it be from five years
old even unto twenty years old, then thy estimation shall
be of the male twenty shekels, and for the female ten
shekels. And if it be from a month old even unto five
years old, then thy estimation shall be of the male, five
shekels of silver, and for the female thy estimation shall
be three shekels of silver. And if it be from sixty years
old and upward, if it be a male, then thy estimation
shall be fifteen shekels, and for the female ten shekels"
(vv.3-7); and (3) "if he be poorer than thy estimation,
then he shall be set before the priest, and the priest shall

value him; according to the ability of him that vowed shall the priest value him" (v.8).

Let us notice the vast differences which exist between these two passages. In the Exodus segment all who were numbered—regardless whether male or female, rich or poor—had to give half a shekel of silver, whereas in the Leviticus segment the shekels given vary with the differences in age, sex, and possession. Why are there such differences? It is because Exodus 30.11-16 speaks of *ransom money*, while Leviticus 27.1-8 speaks of the estimation of a *special vow*.

The Value of Salvation

Since Exodus speaks of ransom money, all who are twenty years old and upward, both male and female, must give half a shekel of silver, for this has reference to *salvation*. Each must give half a shekel, otherwise there will be a plague upon him. In applying this to believers today, everyone must have the Son of God in order that his life may be saved. Our positions as sinners saved by grace are of equal value before God.

"Half a shekel" is equivalent to the "two shillings" spoken of in Luke 10.35. Our Lord Jesus has already paid the two shillings for us. And this amount is sufficient to enable us to stay in the inn (that is, to sojourn in this world until the return of our Savior).

"Twenty years old" refers to the year of man's accountability for himself. Hence the teaching here is that all who are able to bear responsibility for themselves must have the Son of God. With respect to the children of Israel, the year of accountability was counted according to their physical age; in the dispensation of saving grace, no one really knows what is the age of accountability. Some may reach this age of responsibility when they are but seven or eight years old.

"The rich shall not give more, and the poor shall not give less." Since the precious blood of our Lord is the payment, there can be no differentiation between the rich and the poor. Rich or poor may be applied to man's works. People cannot save themselves either by doing good or by doing bad. All must present half a shekel. The salvation which the Lord has accomplished can neither be added on to nor taken away from. All need to be saved through the precious blood. It is called *precious* blood, because it is of *great* value (1 Peter 1.19). The precious blood is a *costly* price, which our Lord Jesus himself has paid for us.

The Estimation of a Special Vow

We notice that the estimation of a special vow was at least six times more than the value of a soul ransomed, for the least amount to be given was three shekels (Lev. 27.6). The most to be given in estimation of a special vow was one hundred times more because some had to give as much as fifty shekels (v.3). Why was there this vast difference? It is because the Exodus passage speaks of *salvation* whereas the Leviticus passage speaks of *consecration*.

Consecration in this connection does not refer to how much I am willing to offer; rather, it refers to *how valuable God looks upon what I am willing to give.*

From the standpoint of salvation, God reckons *every one of us* to be worth half a shekel. No one is valued more than the other. Whether rich or poor, old or young—all have the same value placed upon them by the Lord. What belongs to the natural is all being set aside by God. What saves us is the Son of God. And no one can add anything to or subtract from the Son of God. So that according to grace, each one is as sinful before God as the other, and all have the same ransom price. For Christ's sake, God considers all of us of equal worth before Him. He treasures us; He counts us valuable. But this value is to be found only in His Son, and therefore the value we come into through salvation is the same for each of us in God's sight.

Nevertheless, this does not, in another sense, inhibit God from reckoning some believers to be more valuable than others. Although all are equally saved and all equally become children of God, some may be estimated to be of more value to God than others because their consecration is more complete and their spiritual usefulness is greater. Just here let us take note of these two important factors: that of spiritual usefulness, and that of hearty consecration. It is for these two reasons that God will reckon us as valuable. If a believer has spiritual usefulness but is not consecrated, he has no other value before God than that which he obtains through Christ. Yet if he is willing to offer himself with a pure heart, he will have *some additional value* before God even though he may be only a month to five years old. What is most terrible is for a believer to be worth not a cent more than half a shekel before God: he has the ransom money of half a shekel which guarantees him salvation, but he has nothing more to offer before God.

Let us note that among the children of Israel, people were classified into four age periods: from one month to five years old—childhood; from five years old to twenty years old—youth; from twenty years old to sixty years old—adulthood; from sixty years old and above—decline. In relation to the children of Israel, these were actual *physical* years; but in relation to Christian believers, these point to the variations in *spiritual* strength.

So far as salvation is concerned, all believers are valued the same; but so far as consecration is concerned, it varies with the individual. Each saved person ought to have *some actual value.* God's estimation of one month to five years old was either three shekels (for female) or five shekels (for male). So that in spiritual terms, one who is newly saved should have at least a little worth. And this value, let us keep in mind, comes from consecration. Without consecration, a person is without actual value in God's sight. The work of the Holy Spirit in a saved person is to lead him to consecrate himself that he may live for God. The age period of the five-year-olds to twenty-year-olds may be applied spiritually to those young believers who are zealous and who also have some spiritual experience. And the adulthood age period can be applicable to those strong and experienced believers.

Let us note, though, that the Hebrew people sixty years old and above had their estimation decreased. Yet it need not have been, for let us look at the case of

Caleb. Although he was far advanced in age, his strength remained as it had been in his youth (see Joshua 14.11). Furthermore, "they shall still bring forth fruit in old age," says the psalmist; "they shall be full of sap and green" (92.14). All this would indicate to us that the matured age should be the *best* years. Our spiritual life need not become aged. Unfortunately, however, there can be, and often is, decline in the latter years. Do not incorrectly assume that the estimation we have before God today will last forever. Our spiritual life in terms of value to the Lord has the possibility of declining.

The value estimation for the ages from twenty years old to sixty years old was higher than for any other period, and this class of people, significantly, was mentioned first in this passage. And why? Because from twenty years old and upward they were able to go forth to war (Num. 1.3). When God numbered the twelve tribes of Israel as recorded in Numbers 1, He counted the number of those twenty years old and upward who were able to go forth to war. And so will He similarly evaluate His children of today. All who will consecrate themselves shall be of value. Even the weakest has some value. And those who will stand up for the glory of God, who with God will destroy sin, and who will fight against Satan for God's right are far more valuable in His sight than other believers. Unquestionably, the eyes of God are upon these warriors.

Why, though, is there a difference in estimation between male and female? In our day this is not according to the flesh (though with the Israelites it *was* something physical), but rather it is according to the strength or weakness of spiritual life (cf. 1 Peter 3.7). It is possible for a Christian who has believed the Lord for only one year to be more advanced than he who has already believed for five years.

From this brief discussion we now know that Christians do differ in spiritual age. There is a possibility for decline as well as for advance. Where are *you* at this present moment?

"But if he be poorer than thy estimation, then he shall be set before the priest, and the priest shall value him; according to the ability of him that vowed shall the priest value him" (v.8). What does this mean for today? According to our spiritual age, we ought to give such and such; yet under the enlightenment of the Holy Spirit, we discover we have nothing to match what we *should* give. In that case, we can only come to our great high priest—the Lord Jesus—confessing our inadequacy and asking Him to re-estimate us. We will have to start afresh.

Finally, it is important to note that the shekel was according to *"the shekel of the sanctuary"* (v.3). This meant that an Israelite was worth only that which *God* declared he was worth; and such was unquestionably the most accurate estimation. Human estimation often erred, but the shekel of the sanctuary was most exact. So that what God estimates concerning us believers today is perfect.

We have already had given to us at great cost to the Lord Jesus half a shekel for our initial salvation. Yet today we should inquire of God, saying, "O God, how much more am I worth in your sight?" May our value to Him increase with an ever increasing consecration!

8 | The Love of Christ

Who shall separate us from the love of Christ? shall tribulation, or anguish, or persecution, or famine, or nakedness, or peril, or sword? Even as it is written, For thy sake we are killed all the day long; we were accounted as sheep for the slaughter. Nay, in all these things we are more than conquerors through him that loved us. For I am persuaded, that neither death, nor life, nor angels, nor principalities, nor things present, nor things to come, nor powers, nor height, nor depth, nor any other creation, shall be able to separate us from the love of God, which is in Christ Jesus our Lord. (Rom. 8.35-39 mg.)

The love of Christ constraineth us; because we thus judge, that one died for all, therefore all died; and he died for all, that they that live should no longer live unto themselves, but unto him who for their sakes died and rose again. (2 Cor. 5.14,15)

For this cause I bow my knees unto the Father, from whom every family in heaven and on earth is named, that he would grant you, according to the riches of his glory, that ye may be strengthened with power through his Spirit in the inward man; that Christ may dwell in your hearts through faith; to the end that ye, being rooted and grounded in love, may be strong to apprehend with all the saints what is the breadth and length and height and depth, and to know the love of Christ which passeth knowledge, that ye may be filled unto all the fulness of God. (Eph. 3.14-19)

In these three passages there is one phrase common to all of them: "the love of Christ." Although the Bible speaks much on this theme, it most distinctively mentions the love of Christ only these three times, while the rest speak of the love of God. Yet the Bible makes clear to us that actually the love of God *is* the love of Christ. For although in Romans 8.35 it asks "Who shall separate us from the love of Christ?", in verse 39 of the same passage it concludes with the statement that nothing "shall be able to separate us from the love of God." So that the love of God and the love of Christ are two in one. Nevertheless, we want to discuss specifically "the love of Christ" in relation to three kinds of people.

One—The Love of Christ in Romans 8 Is for the Suffering Ones

Every believer in this world has his particular experiences, problems and environments. But according to Paul, whatever your special situation may be, the "love of Christ" is always the answer. You may have a hundred problems, yet the solution to all of them is the love of Christ. Some believers may incur tribulation, some may encounter poverty, some may meet with persecutions, and some may even suffer abject hunger. Yet, should even nakedness or peril or sword or famine come our way, nothing can separate us from the love of Christ because His love will solve all such difficulties. When a person is gripped by the love of Christ, he is able to go through what many people usually cannot undergo.

A certain widow lived in poverty after the death of her husband. She pawned away all her belongings and she also owed her rent. Yet despite such misery, she still maintained a smiling face. When did she smile? She smiled whenever she saw her child of less than one year old. She smiled because of love.

I treasure the word of Romans 8.37, which says: "Nay, in all these things we are more than conquerors." More than conquerors *in* all these things, not outside all these things. Without these things coming to us, there would be no need to conquer. Many think they can conquer if there is no tribulation, no distress and no persecution. But the word of God declares that we are more than conquerors in all these things. It is the love of Christ that causes us to overcome tribulation, or anguish, or persecution, or famine, or nakedness, or peril, or sword. For the love of Christ is the power that enables us to conquer all these things. All these things are rather painful, nonetheless those who have tasted the love of Christ do not find them so.

Two—The Love of Christ in 2 Corinthians 5 Is for the Servants

This "love of Christ" mentioned here is for those who serve the Lord: "the love of Christ constraineth us" who serve, said Paul (v.14a). The word "constrain" in the Greek original has the idea in it of something being washed away by the water. Hence the love of Christ can be likened to the power of water washing you away. David Livingstone once said that if people came to Africa for the sake of the slave trade, could not and would not the love of Christ constrain a person to go to Africa too? So, he himself went to Africa. Due to that one man who was constrained by the love of Christ to lay down his life, numberless people received divine life. Only the love of Christ can constrain us. Love is something which cannot be displayed, yet all who have tasted the sweetness of it cannot help but be washed away by its power.

"Because we thus judge, that one died for all, therefore all died; and he died for all, that they that live should no longer live unto themselves, but unto him who for their sakes died and rose again" (vv.14b,15). The word "judge" means "conclude." The love of Christ constrains us as we make our judgment in two matters. *One* is, that Christ died for all. His love and His death cannot be separated. We have the love of Christ because He has died. And *two* is, that they who live should no longer live for themselves but to Him who for their sakes died and rose again. This is the end, the conclusion to the matter. Being constrained by the love of Christ, I cannot stand in my old position and not live for Him.

Frequently we find it so hard to witness to a sinner. Before we open our mouth, we are already blushing. When I was first saved, I tried to witness to a schoolmaster. But when I saw him I could hardly speak. It seemed so difficult to open my mouth and talk about Jesus. Nevertheless, as one is constrained by the love of Christ, he cannot but witness. Let us praise and thank the Lord because His love is able to constrain us.

Oftentimes it seems difficult to preach. Hunger and persecution are things which cannot be avoided. Once I had people pointing a gun at me, forbidding me to preach Jesus. But I would rather be shot than not to speak about Christ, for His love has carried me away. I frequently persuade young believers to consecrate themselves to the Lord. This is because of His loving us. Many brothers ask what they should do in order to devote their lives to the preaching of the gospel. Unless you truly feel — as did Paul — that "woe is unto me, if I preach not the gospel" (1 Cor. 9.16), it would be better if you did not become a preacher. Unless necessity is laid upon you, people will not be affected. In preaching the gospel, we must be washed away by the love of Christ. I would not persuade all to be preachers, but I do insist that every believer must witness for the Lord. Let me ask, have you ever told people of the love of Christ? Have you ever felt the love of God burning within you so that you cannot but speak of His love? May the love of Christ fill us today to constrain us.

Three—The Love of Christ in Ephesians 3 Is for the Learner

"For this cause I bow my knees unto the Father, . . . that Christ may dwell in your hearts through faith; to the end that ye, being rooted and grounded in love, may be strong to apprehend with all the saints what is the breadth and length and height and depth, and to know the love of Christ which passeth knowledge, that ye may be filled unto all the fulness of God" (vv.14,17-19). Here "the love of Christ" mentioned is for a learner. Paul is a learned man who can hardly make a grammatical error or compose an ungrammatical sentence. All his letters in the New Testament are written in excellent Greek. Nevertheless, when in Ephesians 3 he writes about the love of Christ, he commits a serious grammatical error. For he stops at the phrase "to apprehend with all the saints" and suddenly writes down "breadth and length and height and depth" (in the original, there is no "what is"). It appears that there is no connection between the preceeding words and the words that follow. This is indeed reflective of the true condition when speaking of the love of Christ. As Paul is writing up to this point, he does not know how further to set down what is on his heart, so he exclaims: "breadth and length and height and depth." He cannot describe it. Yet this provides a far better understanding to people than should a description of the love of Christ be written down in the best of grammar and style. Whenever we think upon the love of Christ, we are at a loss as to what to say, for it appears that the mind is almost useless at that point!

"To know" means the same as "to apprehend." The love of Christ is unknowable and yet it is also knowable. Day by day we learn on this earth a little more concerning the breadth and length and height and depth of the love of Christ. Once, a preacher, while speaking experienced a kind of pressure within him so that he could not say what he wanted to say. He asked the audience for prayer. While people were praying, a black man prayed continually, "Precious Jesus!" That preacher heard this prayer for over an hour. Subsequently he said to his audience, "I have no sermon to preach today; yet from among all your prayers I heard but one word— "Precious Jesus!"

Being constrained by the love of Christ, we love Him though we have not seen Him. By faith we know He is precious.

9 | The Mind of Christ

If there is therefore any exhortation in Christ, if any consolation of love, if any fellowship of the Spirit, if any tender mercies and compassions, make full my joy, that ye be of the same mind, having the same love, being of one accord, of one mind; doing nothing through faction or through vain-glory, but in lowliness of mind each counting other better than himself; not looking each of you to his own things, but each of you also to the things of others. Have this mind in you, which was also in Christ Jesus: who, existing in the form of God, counted not the being on an equality with God a thing to be grasped, but emptied himself, taking the form of a servant, being made in the likeness of men; and being found in fashion as a man, he humbled himself, becoming obedient even unto death, yea, the death of the cross. Wherefore also God highly exalted him, and gave unto him the name which is above every name; that in the name of Jesus every knee should bow, of things in heaven and things on earth and things under the earth, and that every tongue should con-

fess that Jesus Christ is Lord, to the glory of God the
Father. (Phil. 2.1-11)

For the past few weeks this portion of Scripture has
been very much on my heart. As a matter of fact, this
passage is what we Christians must pay constant attention to. Let us consider together this portion of God's
word for a few minutes.

"If there is therefore any exhortation in Christ, if
any consolation of love, if any fellowship of the Spirit,
if any tender mercies and compassions" (v.1). At a
glance this verse does not seem to inspire much thought,
and many who read it do not derive much from it. But
let me say that this verse is most meaningful. For the
realization of the succeeding verses in our lives depends
very much on an understanding of this initial verse.
These opening words of the passage may be deemed
the "soil" for all the other verses. A seed cannot be sown
in the air because it has nowhere to be rooted there.
It must be sown in soil deep and fertile enough for its
growth. And that is why this verse serves as the
necessary soil for the following verses. It furnishes the
nutrients as well as the water for later growth. Without
this verse, then, the rest of this Scripture portion will
be extremely difficult to implement in our lives.

"If there is therefore any [thing] ... in Christ."
These words of Paul are exceedingly important. What
he means is this: if there is any exhortation in Christ,
then we will naturally be of the same mind: if there is
any consolation of love in Christ, it will be easy for
us to have the same love: if there is any fellowship of

the Holy Spirit and if there be any tender mercies, and compassions in the heart, it will be possible to be of one accord and of one mind. On the other hand, though, if there be no exhortation nor consolation of love nor fellowship of the Spirit nor any tender mercies and compassions, then how *can* there be the same mind, the same love, the same accord? In other words, if these things are in Christ, the rest will just naturally follow; otherwise, nothing will be possible.

Do you have any exhortation in Christ, any consolation of love, any fellowship of the Spirit, any tender mercies, and compassions? If you lack these, then how can you expect to practice the things mentioned in the verses that follow? But once having the exhortation, consolation, fellowship, tender mercies, and compassions in Christ, it is most easy for you to be of the same mind and of the same love. And thus the joy of our Lord will be full.

Paul lays out this first verse as the source, the foundation, and the "fertilizer" or "nutrient." If in the absence of this first verse Paul should set about exhorting the brethren at Philippi to be of the same mind and of the same love, to be of one accord and of one love, to be without faction or vainglory but instead to be in lowliness of mind and to be looking after the things of others, how would they respond to him? They would probably say something like this: "Sir, as good as these things you have told us are, we cannot do them. Only Christ can. Yet we do not have the power of Christ because we belong to the world. How can we possibly achieve these things? We may indeed love the lovable, but we find it hard to love the unlovely. And I have my own thought, and someone else has his own idea. So how *can* we be of one mind?" It is for this reason that Paul prepared the way for the Philippian brethren to enter into the reality of the succeeding verses by first laying down the prerequisite condition in verse 1. In that verse he told them the secret: "If there is any [thing] . . . in Christ," then all will be easy. In order to be full, food must be taken in; in order to have strength, power needs to be supplied first. A brother put it well when he observed: "People exhort others to put out strength, but I advise them to put in strength." How can strength be expended if it is not first taken in? And that is exactly what this verse calls for. Paul shows us that there *is* the necessary power in Christ. *"In Christ"* — Oh! how significant is this phrase! For only in Him can we do all things. Outside of Christ, we are sinners; but in Christ, we are saved. Outside of Christ, we are defeated; but in Christ, we are victorious.

"Make full my joy, that ye be of the same mind, having the same love, being of one accord, of one mind" (v.2). As a result of the supply cited in the first verse, we can experience the reality of this second verse. Because there is this source of power in Christ, therefore one mind can be a reality here.

Can there be the same mind? the same love? Once I asked a brother in Foochow the process whereby we two would be of the same mind. Would it be necessary for me to change my mind to his or for him to change his mind to mine? Now it *might* be possible with two persons, but what if there were *three* people involved? How could two people's minds be changed to the mind of the third person? And supposing there were five or five hundred or a thousand people involved, how could so many minds become the same? Yet according to Paul it would appear to be very easy for all to arrive at the same mind. For the apostle, it is simply as verse 5 suggests: "Have this mind in you, which was also in Christ Jesus." The solution to the problem is not to be found in the formula whereby I am to lay aside my mind in deference to yours nor by you laying aside your mind in deference to mine. It is instead achieved by our placing the mind of Christ in the midst and allowing both of us to be of the same mind *with Him*. If every mind is to be of the same mind as Christ's, then it is a matter of all of us simply having the same mind in spite of the great number of people involved. When we are attempting to undertake something, it is quite likely that you will have your thought and I will have mine. Should you, then, submit to me, or should it be that I must submit to you? Some people may think that perhaps the other person should submit. But this is not God's way. His way is to "have this mind in you which was also in Christ Jesus."

What loss it will be to God if any brother or sister should go astray and refuse to obey the Lord! Were we of the same mind, it would give God joy—yea, much joy; for here in this verse 2 Paul is representing the Lord's heart. The heart of the Lord will be full of joy if believers are of one mind. A number of things can indeed gladden the Lord's heart, but the one accord of Christians will make him full of joy. Winning souls will give the Lord joy; victorious living will also give Him joy; but having one mind will alone give Him *great* joy.

Such oneness is internal as well as external. God can so work in us that we are not only one in speech but also one in heart.

Some people's oneness is merely in their mouths because their hearts are not really one. Even though their hearts are so far apart, and their attitudes betray the fact that they are not of one accord with other people, they can still declare they are one. Such oneness is not that which is spoken of here. Only on the basis of "if there is ... in Christ" can there be any one-mindedness.

"Doing nothing through faction or through vainglory, but in lowliness of mind each counting other better than himself" (v.3). This is still based on Paul's understanding of the phrase "in Christ." What is faction? Factionalism denotes the taking of sides. Instead of the Lord, someone else becomes your goal. When two persons are at odds, for example, you declare that you are for one of them. But this is wrong. You can only stand on the Lord's side, or else you will fall into factionalism.

What kind of glory is vainglory? The Scriptures at one point speak of "an eternal weight of glory" (2 Cor. 4.17). Glory is weighty and substantial, therefore it sinks to the bottom, not floating on the top. Such weight of glory can only be seen by God. What is apparent and seen by many people is something vainglorious. What does a person obtain from such vainglory? Nothing but a lusting, for who can ever obtain that which is vain and empty? All he can do is to lust continually after it.

Sometimes unfortunate strife occurs among brothers and sisters. If this is not due to faction, then it usually is because of seeking after vainglory. Each desires to be great; none is willing to give in. Actually, desiring greatness will not make one great; there will always be someone greater.

When one is being praised and honored he seems to be glorified, whereas in fact his feet tread on floating clouds. We need to remember that all glories which come from men are but *vain*glories. Once a renowned English scholar wrote a famous novel. One day he was invited to a feast by a duke. At the table, a woman of nobility profusely praised his novel. The author stood up and said to the woman that she was not qualified to praise his book. He considered her praise to be disgraceful. Who, then, is worthy to praise us? Apart from our Lord, no one is worthy. When we are praised by men, we have already been downgraded, so why should we lust after it? We will not accept men's praise nor seek for such praise if our mind is set on the future and our heart seeks to hear *the Lord* say, "Well done, good and faithful servant" (Matt. 25.21).

Not only should we, negatively, refrain from pursuing after vainglory, we should also, positively, "in lowliness of mind count others better than ourselves." What is lowliness? Lowliness means reserving no place for oneself. He who reserves a place for himself is never lowly in mind. He who claims he has authority and deserves to get something is not humble. One may speak humbly, but he may not be lowly in mind. It may come through the mouth, but it may not pass out of the heart.

Where does lowliness of mind express itself? It is expressed through the attitude of "counting others better than oneself." Such is the unmistakable hallmark of lowliness. How difficult it is to count others better than oneself! Once I met an elderly believer who had served the Lord for many decades. A brother asked him which was the most difficult of all Christian virtues. His answer was Philippians 2.3: "In lowliness of mind each counting other better than himself." Yes, indeed, it is exceedingly hard to have lowliness of mind. For what sin turned the archangel Lucifer into Satan? Was it not pride? He fell because he wanted to be equal with the Most High. What sin caused man to become a sinner? Was it not also pride? Adam ate the forbidden fruit, expecting to know good and evil as did God. He ate, and he fell terribly. Hence humility is truly the hardest to attain to of all the virtues. Possibly no one on earth has ever fully attained to it. We can find people with ability or eloquence, but where can we find a truly humble person?

How can we count the other person better than ourselves? One believer has said it well: "See the old man in myself, and see the new man in the other." If we truly look at our natural life and perceive how corrupted we are, and then look at the other person and discern how the grace of God has transformed him, we cannot help but count the other better than ourselves. The believers in Rome should receive help from Paul, yet Paul expected their help because their faith was at that time being proclaimed throughout the entire world (Rom. 1.8). He expected to be comforted by the new work of God in their midst during his anticipated visit with them in the future (1.12,13ff.).

I had a conversation with a woman missionary on the following point: Who demands more—the Lord towards the believers or the believers towards the Lord? I thought that the Lord would probably demand more. We who are so imperfect often make great demands on people and have great expectations of them; surely, then, the Lord who is perfect would make even greater demands and have even greater expectations. To my surprise she said no to my notion. I asked for her reason. Her answer was that we believers see the apparent failures of people, but the Lord sees their hidden victories. I confess that this word came out of deep experience, for I have since learned how true this that she said is. What *we* see is somebody who has *failed* once, twice, or many times; but what *the Lord* sees is someone who has secretly *overcome* once, twice, perhaps even a hundred times. You yourself may be tempted five times and you fail those five times, whereas quite possibly the other person may be tempted three times but he only fails once. He may experience many victories in secret which you cannot see and which you do not experience yourself. You may wage *ten* battles and lose once, but he may fight a *hundred* battles and only lose twice. If only we could understand this we would be more inclined to count others better than ourselves.

"Not looking each of you to his own things, but each of you also to the things of others" (v.4). This is something not easy to implement. Due to my poor health in recent years, I have been unable to look after the things of others very much. Frequently we feel we neither have time nor energy to take care of our own things, so how can we possibly take care of others' affairs. To look after the things of others is truly a self-denying life. I once met a missionary with the China

Inland Mission. I asked her if she had ever seen Hudson Taylor in person and what she felt was his distinctive characteristic. She replied that so far as she knew, the one most distinctive characteristic of the man was that whenever anyone went to see him, he seemed to have nothing to do but to consider that person's affairs as the most important business at hand. Actually he wrote many letters and interviewed numerous people each day. Yet he appeared as though he had only others' affairs to take care of. This is truly self-denial. If our Lord were as cold and careless to others as we are, where would we be today? Where would I be? Our Lord indeed cares only for the things of others; for did He not die for us because we had sinned? Let us therefore be taught by this profound example to care for the things of others.

"Have this mind in you, which was also in Christ Jesus" (v.5). This statement is actually a summing up of the preceding four verses. Everything will be fine and nothing will be impossible if we have the mind of Christ. What is the mind of Christ? Paul gives his classic definition in verses 6 to 8 that follow.

"Who, existing in the form of God, counted not the being on an equality with God a thing to be grasped, but emptied himself, taking the form of a servant, being made in the likeness of men" (vv.6,7). The prerogatives of Christ — that which is legally and rightfully His — is His being in the form of God and being equal with God. Yet He "emptied himself, taking the form of a servant, being made in the likeness of men." What, then, you ask, is the mind of Christ? It is to do what He did: to forfeit one's rightful privileges. Perhaps you are concerned about how you should be treated by other people. But Christ does not hold on to what is rightfully His. He took the attitude of mind that His being on an equality with God was not something to be grasped after, but instead He emptied himself and took the form of a bondslave. Such is the mind of Christ.

How we dwell on having our lawful privileges. Nevertheless, our Lord observed this: "Ye know that the rulers of the Gentiles lord it over them, and their great ones exercise authority over them. Not so shall it be among you" (Matt. 20.25,26a). Moreover, the teaching of Jesus found in Matthew 5-7 may be summed up in two succinct statements: Forsake what rightfully belongs to you, and, Accept gladly what is not your due. Other people may return eye for eye and tooth for tooth, but the Lord says to pray for those who persecute you. Lay down what is rightfully yours and take up what is unworthy for you—such is the sum total of the law and the prophets. Whether at home or abroad, no Christian should speak of his rights. Had our Lord argued among the Godhead as to whether or not the Father could send Him, would the Father have ever been able to send Him? On the one hand Jesus said, "I and the Father are one" (John 10.30); on the other hand He also said this: "the Father is greater than I" (John 14.28). Is there any inherent gradation of power and authority between and among the members in the Godhead? Certainly not. And hence the consideration of greater or smaller here cannot have reference to that which one is born with; rather, it is something that is willed or desired or submitted to gladly. The Father sends the Son, and the Son sends the Spirit. And such a submissive arrangement is according to the sublime humility to be found in the Godhead.

"The form of a servant" are words which speak of the lowliness of our Lord; "the likeness of men" is a phrase which signifies the human restriction our Lord takes upon himself. The form of a servant is presented in contrast to the form of God, while man is presented in contrast to God. God is not restricted by time and space, by food and rest. The form of God is glorious, whereas the form of a servant is lowly. The mind of Christ is therefore expressed in His willingness to humble himself and to suffer restriction.

"And being found in fashion as a man, he humbled himself, becoming obedient even unto death, yea, the death of the cross" (v.8). The obedience of Christ is profoundly demonstrated in His obeying His *equal, not* in His obeying His *superior.* His obedience is from the heart and goes all the way to the death of the cross.

We Christians ought to be more loving and more at peace with one another. The way described in verses 6-8 is truly the way of the cross. Any brother or sister who has not learned to deny self, to lay down legal rights, and to humble himself or herself among his or her equals, has never traveled along this way of the cross. Once a missionary made a significant comment. A certain brother, she observed, is always exhorting people to walk the way of the cross, to tread the narrow way; yet I have noticed, she added, that he himself has not even stepped through its gate! How true it is that unless we have denied ourselves, we have not entered upon the way of the cross. How we wish to choose the way of the cross, yet we fail to realize that it lies in the denying of self and in dying daily.

A sister in the Lord met a physician who was very active in the assembly. This learned physician was knowledgeable in the word of God and eloquent in preaching. Yet this sister one day told him, "Sir, you preach well, but you walk wrongly." "I preach the way of the cross," replied the physician, "for we all need to deny ourselves and take up the cross." "Indeed," said the sister; "but I notice that you yourself have never died." The physician humbly asked for help; and the sister spoke to him quite frankly according to God's word. Sometime later, he wrote a letter to that sister, in which he said: "After you left, I told God that I neither knew what the cross was, nor what the way of the cross was, nor what denying self was. But, with my ignorance I offer myself to You, Lord, and ask You to enable me to deny myself. Then, my problem came. My wife began to oppose me. When I could no longer endure, I heard a voice saying to me, Deny self and die to these things. Previously, I had often spoken of the cross and of self-denial and of death to self, though I really did not know when or where or how I should die to myself. Now, however, I know how to make it work out in life; for whenever I now speak on this matter, many people oppose me. Even my medical practice has suffered. I now know that I need to die among my own contemporaries."

Many know the truth and know they must deny self. But where are they to die? As this physician discovered, they must begin to die to themselves among their very contemporaries. We must die among people we daily see and touch. May God bless us that we may fill the Lord's heart with joy because we are "of the same mind, having the same love, being of one accord, of one mind"—in Christ.

TITLES YOU
WILL WANT TO HAVE

By Watchman Nee

CD ROM – Complete works of Nee by CFP

Basic Lesson Series
Volume 1 – A Living Sacrifice
Volume 2 – The Good Confession
Volume 3 – Assembling Together
Volume 4- Not I, But Christ
Volume 5 – Do All to the Glory of God
Volume 6 – Love One Another

The Church and the Work
Volume 1 – Assembly Life
Volume 2 – Rethinking the Work
Volume 3 – Church Affairs
Revive Thy Work
The Word of the Cross
The Communion of the Holy Spirit
The Finest of the Wheat – Volume 1
The Finest of the Wheat – Volume 2
Take Heed
Worship God
Interpreting Matthew
The Character of God's Workman
Gleanings in the Fields of Boaz
The Spirit of the Gospel
The life That Wins
From Glory to Glory
The Spirit of Judgment
From Faith to Faith
Back to the Cross
The Lord My Portion
Aids to "Revelation"
Grace for Grace
The Better Covenant
A Balanced Christian Life
The Mystery of Creation

The Messenger of the Cross
Full of Grace and Truth – Volume 1
Full of Grace and Truth – Volume 2
The Spirit of Wisdom and Revelation
Whom Shall I Send?
The Testimony of God
The Salvation of the Soul
The King and the Kingdom of Heaven
The Body of Christ: A Reality
Let Us Pray
God's Plan and the Overcomers
The Glory of His Life
"Come, Lord Jesus"
Practical Issues of This Life
Gospel Dialogue
God's Work
Ye Search the Scriptures
The Prayer Ministry of the Church
Christ the Sum of All Spiritual Things
Spiritual Knowledge
The Latent Power of the Soul
The Ministry of God's Word
Spiritual Reality or Obsession
The Spiritual Man
The Release of The Spirit
Spiritual Authority

By Stephen Kaung

Discipled to Christ
The Splendor of His Ways
Seeing the Lord's End in Job
The Songs of Degrees
Meditations on Fifteen Psalms

ORDER FROM:

Christian Fellowship Publishers, Inc.
11515 Allecingie Parkway
Richmond, Virginia 23235